Praise for

TREASURES FOR
WOMEN WHO HOPE

"Alice Gray knows how to point people to irresistible hope! The suggestions for discussion and journaling provide personal application for every reader. If you have a friend walking through an experience that makes no sense, you now have the perfect gift—*Treasures for Women Who Hope*. This timeless book will be one of your favorites!"

> — **Carol Kent**
> Speaker and best-selling author,
> *When I Lay My Isaac Down*

"Life isn't always easy. Although there are twists and turns along the way, God often provides hope and comfort through the stories of others. In her new book, *Treasures for Women Who Hope*, Alice Gray leads us to the shelter of God's love through stories of strength and hope both from her own life and that of others. You will be encouraged and blessed as you read of God's grace and power at work in the lives of women who found their hope in Him."

> — **Karol Ladd**
> Speaker and best-selling author,
> *A Positive Plan for Creating More
> Calm, Less Stress*

"Alice Gray has done something very powerful with this book. She shares stories of hope in the midst of difficulty; truths that shine like candles in the darkness, giving light when it is most needed. During times that the darkness seems overwhelming, I crave encouragement from others who have been there. In this book, Alice has collected just that sort of encouragement in one place. I am so grateful for a resource that can help me and others when we need that touch from heaven."

> — **Shaunti Feldhahn**
> Speaker and best-selling author,
> *For Women Only*

"I can't begin to express how much this book has meant to me. I find myself looking at the chapters not only through my eyes and experience, but also through the eyes of other women in my ministry sphere. I know they will benefit immensely from what Alice has written. Her words have encouraged my heart and lifted the clouds hanging over my spirit."

— Karen
Pastor's wife and women's
ministry mentor

"I truly love what Alice has written; it spoke to my heart. I can hardly wait for this book to be published so I can share it with my ladies at Bible study—so many are going through the experiences she writes about."

— Nancy
Bible study teacher

"Reading *Treasures for Women Who Hope* is like sitting down with Alice, sharing a hug and a steaming cup of tea. Her heart for the situations women struggle with shows on every page...she knows and she cares."

— Doreen
Wife, mom, and student

"One of God's greatest gifts to the believer is hope. The door to joy is closed when we misplace our hope. *Treasures for Women Who Hope* helps to open that door and remind us anew of this special gift."

— Nancy
Pastor's wife

"What a blessing to settle back into a comfortable chair and 'listen' to a friend share words of hope and inspiration. Alice has reminded me that faith is having complete trust in God and that what happens is His good choice for me even when I don't understand."

— Elizabeth
Women's ministry director

"Alice's writing style has such broad appeal and her attitude is so very gracious, encouraging, and genuine. It often feels very lonely when going through hard times. It helps to know that others are going through storms, too. Knowing that you aren't alone helps you to persevere."

— Patti
Stay-at-home mother of four

Treasures for Women Who Hope

TREASURES FOR WOMEN WHO HOPE

Alice Gray

W PUBLISHING GROUP
A Division of Thomas Nelson Publishers
Since 1798

www.wpublishinggroup.com

Published by W Publishing Group, P.O. Box 141000, Nashville, Tennessee 37214, a division of Thomas Nelson, Inc.

W Publishing Group books may be purchased in bulk for educational, business, fundraising, or sales promotional use. For information, please e-mail SpecialMarkets@ThomasNelson.com.

Unless otherwise noted, Scripture quotations are from The New King James Version, copyright 1979, 1980, 1982, Thomas Nelson, Inc., Publishers.

Other translations used in this book are from the following:

The King James Version of the Bible.

The Holy Bible, New International Version. Copyright © 1973, 1978, 1984, International Bible Society. Used by permission of Zondervan Bible Publishers.

The *Holy Bible*, New Living Translation copyright ©1996 by Tyndale Charitable Trust. Used by permission of Tyndale House Publishers, Inc., Wheaton, Illinois 60189. All rights reserved.

The Message, copyright © 1993. Used by permission of NavPress Publishing Group. All rights reserved.

New American Standard Bible, ©1960, 1977 by the Lockman Foundation.

Library of Congress Cataloging-in-Publication Data

Gray, Alice.
    Treasures for women who hope.
      p. cm.
    ISBN 0-8499-0437-4
    1. Christian women—Religious life. 2. Hope—Religious aspects—Christianity.
3. Christian life—Anecdotes. I. Gray, Alice, 1939–
BV4527.T74 2005
242'.643—dc22   2005014149

Printed in the United States of America

05 06 07 08 09 RRD 6 5 4 3 2 1

For my mother,
who taught me how to hope

Contents

A Special Thank-You . . .

To my friends—some new and some forever—
Doreen Button, Karen L. Ellison, Nancy Harris,
Elizabeth D. Hightower, Patti Killgore, Nancy Larson,
Darla A. Smith.
*Thank you for previewing the manuscript. Your prayers,
comments, and notes of encouragement always arrived
just when I needed them the most.*

To my editor, Anne Christian Buchanan.
*Thank you for dusting the pages with your magic and
making my writing so much better. It's an honor to work
with the best of the best.*

To my husband, Al Gray.
*Thank you for your strong and tender care through all the
years. I love it that we both hope for the same things.*

To my Lord and Savior, Jesus Christ.
*Thank You for being the Hope that never disappoints.
I pray this book brings pleasure to You.*

A Note to My Readers

I have used many true stories in this book, but unless I had specific permission from the people involved, I changed the names and altered the circumstances to protect their privacy.

WHEN GOD WHISPERS HOPE

*God is the only one who can make
the valley of trouble a door of hope.*

CATHERINE MARSHALL

Dark storm clouds painted the sky a two-toned gray on that bitterly cold November morning in Oregon. Sudden bursts of wind chased all but the last leaves from the trees, exposing their naked limbs to near-freezing temperatures. Pulling my coat tighter around me, I shivered with winter's sudden arrival.

As I opened the door to the little coffee-and-gift shop where I was meeting my friend Marlene, yummy smells of cinnamon and ginger greeted me. The ambience was so warm and welcoming I could almost hear a fire crackling in some cozy corner. I immediately fell in love with the quaint little store, and although this was my first visit, I knew I would return again and again. Such a contrast to the frigid storm that was brewing outside.

I spotted Marlene browsing near the candle display and discovered that the wonderful fragrance drifting through the shop came from a single pillar candle appropriately labeled "Pumpkin Pie." (I would definitely do a little shopping later.) We shared a brief hug, then hurried over to a grouping of small tables next to the gift area. The tables were small, with just two chairs each, and arranged rather closely together. But they were just right for enjoying mochas, cinnamon rolls, and intimate conversation—which is why we were there in the first place.

Marlene and I didn't get together often, so our jaws were flying from the moment we sat down. It's not that we were in a hurry; we just had so much to share about our families and our lives. And it just so happened that, on that particular morning, both of us were experiencing some painful challenges and disappointments. There was good news too, of course. And because we both love Jesus, our conversation was sprinkled with references to the Lord and hope that we would see our prayers answered.

We hadn't paid much attention to the young woman sitting at the table closest to ours, but when we stopped long enough to sip our mochas, my eyes met hers. I was struck by the absolute radiance of her face. Joy bubbled out of what seemed to be a gentle and quiet spirit. Then she smiled and said hello.

She explained that she couldn't help but hear some of our conversation, and she wanted to use the moment to encourage us. She spoke softly, almost in a whisper, simply reminding Marlene and me that God was aware of and concerned with our heartaches and that nothing could ever separate us from His love. She said He was watching over us with gladness in His heart.

Her voice was extraordinarily beautiful—so lovely that Marlene and I commented later that our conversation was like having an encounter with an angel. (Not that either of us had knowingly had an encounter before.) With another reassuring smile, she indicated that she was through talking. She tilted her chin down for a tiny moment, as though she might be saying a brief prayer for us, then returned to reading her book.

Marlene and I continued our conversation. But something was different. We had been refreshed by our unusual encounter.

A short time later, when this young woman got up to leave, I noticed that even though she was smartly dressed, she wore bulky tennis shoes. Then I saw that she walked with a severe limp and carried a walking stick, though she seemed to be trying to walk without it. She held her head high—not proudly, but triumphantly—as she stepped out into the storm.

God Is There

When the sky is dark—
    He is there.
When you are all alone—
    He is there.
When nothing goes your way—
    He is there.
When you are in pain—
    He is there.
When people are against you—
    He is there.
When you are frightened or worried—
    He is there.
When those you love are in crisis—
    He is there.
When you feel as if God is far away—
    He is there.
When doubt and confusion weigh you down—
    He is there.
When you are about to breathe your last—
    He is there.
And where God is, there is always hope.

DR. STEVE STEPHENS[1]

After she left, the waitress told us that our "friend" came in about two times a week for coffee and that she always seemed to find a way to encourage everyone she talked to. The waitress went on to explain about the shoes and the walking stick.

A severe automobile accident had almost killed the young woman a year before. Since then, she had been in and out of the hospital and rehabilitation center. Her husband had divorced her, their home had been sold, and she had just moved into her own apartment. She used public transportation because she still couldn't drive. And though she was currently looking for employment, so far there hadn't been any good prospects.

Marlene and I sat stunned. This young woman's conversation had been filled with delights of the Lord. There had been no weariness about her. She had encouraged us with words of praise and promise. Meeting her that day, we never would have suspected that storms were raging in her life. Even as she stepped outside into the cold winter wind, she'd seemed to carry God's warm shelter of hope with her.

Part of the Journey

As much as we wish we could always have blue skies and smooth sailing, storms are a part of the journey of life. Some of us have public storms—many people are aware of them. Others have storms known by only a few close friends and family. Still others have private storms known only between them and the Lord. Your storms may rage like hurricanes, or they may hit like a sudden downpour on a humid afternoon. Sometimes there is distant thunder first. Sometimes there is no warning at all. Either way, storms can feel scary and uncontrollable. They can shake your confidence or even your faith.

As I begin writing this book on hope, I am already thinking about you, the reader. I'm wondering how the book will come into your hands. Will a friend give it to you or will you purchase it yourself? What is it about the title or the cover that invites you inside its pages?

I'm also thinking about the storms in your life—the worries and sorrows you might be facing—and why the word *hope* might be meaningful to you at the very moment you are reading this page.

I wish we could meet at the same little coffee-and-gift shop where Marlene and I spent that November morning. It would be so good just to sit and talk in the cinnamon-scented quietness while mugs of hot chocolate warmed our hands. Or, if you preferred, we could get together on a summer day and sip lemonade while sitting on a park bench under a canopy of shade trees.

Whatever your favorite spot for intimate conversation, I would like to meet you there. If I placed my hand gently over yours and said simply, "I have time to listen," what would you say? If you could trust me, what hurts would you share?

As your story came tumbling out, would your cheeks be wet with tears because of recent heartbreaks—or would your face show the weariness of someone who has known disappointments and unanswered prayer for too many years? If you described storms that hit suddenly, crashing hard on your life and leaving terrible destruction, I would understand some of the pain behind your words—because I too have experienced these kinds of storms. If you talked about daily problems that linger like heavy gray clouds, always threatening to ruin the sunshine of your days, you would see recognition in my eyes.

Although we cannot have that conversation face to face, I want you to know that I started praying for you even before I started writing this book. Like the woman who spoke to Marlene and me in the quaint little gift shop, I want to be God's messenger reminding you that He cares about what you are going through. While He was forming you in your mother's womb, your heavenly Father already knew everything you would be facing this very day. He knows your joys and strengths and blessings but also your weariness, your sorrows, and your heartaches. He wants you to remember that nothing can ever separate you from His love, that He will fold you in His arms and carry you close to His heart and turn your mourning into joy.[2]

If my prayers are answered, you will let God be your welcoming shelter when storms come. And when you listen for His voice, you will hear God whisper words of hope.

A Look Beyond the Clouds

Do you love stories? I do. Stories have always spoken to my heart in a special way, and in the course of my writing and editing career, I've collected some wonderful ones. I've sprinkled several of my favorites through this book, hoping that you enjoy them as much as I do and that they help you, as they have helped me, to live more hopefully. The first of these is from Emilie Barnes who is perhaps best known for her books about tea and about creating a lovely home. From the first time I picked up Welcome Home *and* The Twelve Teas of Friendship, *her gentle words fell softly and happily on my heart. In another book,* Help Me Trust You, Lord, *Emilie writes about how she found hope during a time of chronic illness. To me, this description of what she learned about hope in the midst of storms feels like walking through tough times with a gentle and loving friend.*

I've seen it a million times in the years that [my husband] Bob and I have been frequent flyers. Every time, it has surprised and delighted me. More recently, it has been a source of comfort and encouragement—a mental picture that has kept me going in the rainy seasons of my life.

Here's how it happens.

We drive to the airport in pouring rain, or dreary drizzle, or gray overcast.

We check our luggage as usual, pass through the gauntlet of X-ray checks, wait at our gate while staring out at the now-familiar wet grayness.

We board the plane, stow our carry-ons, glance out through the rain-spattered windows as we fasten our seatbelts.

Then we take off, disappearing within minutes into a blanket of fog.

We glance at our magazines and listen with half an ear to the familiar litany of safety instructions.

And then, just as we're getting settled into the routine, we glance out the window again to see . . . nothing but blue skies and sunshine.

No matter what the weather is like down on the ground, once you get above those clouds, it's always a sunny day!

And it is beautiful up there. Seen from above, those very clouds that rained on everyone's parade and dragged down everyone's spirits are soft, billowy, inviting. I find myself wanting to jump down into them and bounce around like a child on a wonderful featherbed.

How can the same clouds look so amazingly different?

It's all a matter of perspective . . . and it's a perspective I desperately need on these days when everything seems dark.

My rainy season, you see, is far from over.

My disease is a chronic one; my health will likely improve and then decline and improve and decline, perhaps for the rest of my life. . . . And I have no guarantees that the other kinds of pain in my life are behind me. Neither do you. Neither does any of us.

The Lord [reminded us] that in this world we will have trouble. That's a given, an inevitable consequence of living amidst this fallen creation. The rain falls on the just and the unjust, and one good soaking is no guarantee that we won't get wet again.

But that's why it's so important to keep in mind the truth that I learn and relearn whenever I'm given the privilege of flying above the clouds:

No matter how thick the clouds and how hard the rain, you see, the sun is still shining.

At the very same moment that life seems darkest, the sun is dancing beautifully off those puffy, inviting clouds.

Most important, our Lord and Savior Jesus Christ has promised that the sunshine is the place we belong—and the sun is always shining. . . .

It's so easy to forget that . . . when the storm clouds loom.

It's so easy to become depressed and discouraged when the rainy season lingers. It's so easy to fall into fear when the low places flood.

But it's so vital to remember, again and again, that the sun has never really left us. Rainy seasons come and go, but even the longest rain is still temporary. It's the sunshine that never ends.

EMILIE BARNES
From *Help Me Trust You, Lord*[3]

A Gentle Touch
For discussion or journaling

He tends His flock like a shepherd:
He gathers the lambs in his arms
and carries them close to his heart.

ISAIAH 40:11
NEW INTERNATIONAL VERSION

1. Read through "God Is There" on page xix. Which phrases are most comforting to you today? What statements would you add to the list?

2. If you were getting together with a good friend today, what current joys and blessings could you share? What are some painful disappointments you are facing? What happenings in your life make it hard for you to hope?

3. Describe the last time you felt God whispering hope to you. What would have to happen for you to feel that hope again?

A Prayer from the Heart

Dear Lord,

Help me understand how deeply You love me and how much You care about what I'm going through. You have said that You will tend Your flock like a shepherd and carry the lambs close to Your heart. Encourage me today with the thought that You desire to gather me in Your arms and snuggle me close to You. Please whisper words of hope to me today.

SOMEBODY KNOWS

Hope comes from knowing
I have a sovereign, loving God
who is in every event in my life.

LISA BEAMER,
WIDOW OF TODD BEAMER,
KILLED ON UNITED AIRLINES FLIGHT 93,
SEPTEMBER 11, 2001

My husband, Al, and I live near the Colorado River in a midsized Arizona town that is a winter haven for "snowbirds"—retirees who love the desert sunshine and the idea that they can still wear shorts in December and January. They enjoy the slower pace they find here—we're about thirty miles from the next town and more than a two-hour drive to the closest "big" city. And then, there's the nighttime sky.

You see, none of the neighborhoods in our town have streetlights. They just weren't part of the plan. If you go outside at night and look up, you understand why. Stars seem close enough for touching.

It's no wonder that on many evenings Al and I sit outside on the back patio watching the sky quickly change from a red and purple canvas to a midnight blue canopy that's studded with shimmering stars. Sometimes we stay outside longer than intended just because it's so beautiful.

But last night we lingered for another reason. We were praying for our family and friends . . . and for a week of shattered dreams. I'm not talking about ordinary ups and downs. This week all the news had been frightfully down—struggling marriages, dreaded illnesses, financial hardships, rebellious children. Our hearts were aching, and we sent up prayer after prayer on behalf of those we loved.

Even after praying, we were still reluctant to go back inside. Restless discouragement hovered over us, and we both seemed to be waiting for some sign from God—something tangible—to chase away our gloomy feelings. But the heavens, though beautiful, were silent. We felt like our prayers hadn't reached any higher than the pygmy palm trees.

We sat outside for almost another hour before my husband reached over and took my hand. He wasn't looking at me; he was looking up. With warmth and confidence in his voice, he recited one of our favorite Scripture promises:

> God is our refuge and strength,
> A very present help in trouble.
> Therefore we will not fear.[1]

Remembering this Bible verse and saying it out loud had a profound effect on us. Simply acknowledging God and determining to place our trust in Him provided the assurance we needed that . . .

God knows.

God cares.

Our prayers had reached beyond the stars after all.

God's Voice

In his spiritual memoir *Now and Then*, novelist Frederick Buechner writes that God often speaks to us through the events of our lives. "If we keep our hearts and minds open as well as our ears, if we listen with patience and hope, if we remember at all deeply and honestly, then I think we come to recognize, beyond all doubt, that, however faintly we may hear him, he is indeed speaking to us."[2]

Whenever overwhelming circumstances get the best of me, I find myself trying to listen more intently for God's voice. And as Buechner says, when I listen with patience and hope, I recognize more readily that He is speaking to me. Sometimes His words of encouragement come through the godly counsel of friends and family, sometimes through the wondrous ways of nature, sometimes through the gentle nudgings of the Holy Spirit. But for me, His voice is clearest when I open His love letter, the Bible, and start reading the familiar verses I've marked and others the Lord may lead me to.

Hundreds of Scriptures talk about troubles, and hundreds more give peace when troubles come. The words of some passages calm my heart the way Jesus's voice must have calmed the frightened disciples when He said to the storm, "Peace, be still!"[3] For the rest of this chapter and the next two, I want to focus on just one of these. It's a passage people often turn to when their happiness starts falling away. The words were written by . . .

> *Weave the unveiling fabric of God's Word through your heart and mind. It will hold strong, even if the rest of life unravels.*
>
> GIGI GRAHAM TCHIVIDJIAN

a family man who lost his family,
 a wealthy man who lost his wealth,
  a healthy man who lost his health,
   a man who had everything and lost everything . . .
   everything but hope.

Have you already guessed who I'm talking about? The man is Job, whose remarkable story takes up an entire book in the Old Testament. And the particular verse I'm referring to is Job 23, verse 10:

> But He knows the way that I take;
> When He has tested me,
> I shall come forth as gold.

For me, in those three little lines shines the hope of a thousand stars, the indelible promise that God knows exactly what He is doing in my life—and that it's all for the good.

God Knows the Way I Take

In my Bible, I've circled and underlined the first part of Job 23:10 and drawn a heart around the word *knows*. That word is especially important to me because sometimes I find myself wondering if the One who knows when every sparrow falls to the ground really knows what I am going through. I feel like the little toddler in children's church last Sunday who reached up and turned my cheek in his direction and said, "Teacher, look at me."

Haven't we all wished God was near enough that we could touch His cheek, turn it in our direction, and say, "God, look at me." Perhaps Job felt that way too.

In the verses right before Job 23:10, Job is telling his friends how abandoned he feels because he can't see God. (And so how could God see him?) Job describes how he has searched forward and backward, to the right and to the left, but still he cannot find Him. And this, of course, is after he has lost just about everything.

And yet despite his doubts, Job must still have trusted God's heart. For right in the middle of his forsaken lament, Job makes this incredible statement: "But He knows the way that I take."

At his darkest moment, when the storm was raging and the waves were crashing, Job had an anchor: *God knows about me.*

If you are tossed on the waves of hurt and the circumstances seem pitch black, you have that anchor too. Know that God sees you. He understands what you're going through, and His thoughts of you are precious.[4]

Listen to the words of Psalm 139:1–5, which tenderly describe God's personal involvement in your life:

> O LORD, you . . . know everything about me.
> You know when I sit down or stand up.
>   You know my every thought when far away. . . .
>   Every moment you know where I am. . . .
> You both precede and follow me.
>   You place your hand of blessing on my head.[5]

What a beautiful portrait of a God who is intimately acquainted with all our ways and never goes a moment without thinking of us. If you long to touch God's cheek and say, "Look at me," you can trust that His face is already turned toward you. He is before you, behind you, and over you. You are enclosed by God!

That's an absolutely amazing thought. No wonder the psalmist adds, "Such knowledge is too wonderful for me." It's too wonderful for you and me too—almost impossible to grasp. We really can't comprehend omniscient God or understand how He works. But sometimes we can catch a glimpse of His ways—and hope often lies in those tiny glimpses.

A Tiny Glimpse

Pastor Ron Mehl is one of my favorite authors. He wrote tender books about hard times—books with titles like *Meeting God at a Dead End* and *God Works the Night Shift*. One time I heard Pastor Ron give an illustration that helped me get an ever-so-small and ever-more-hopeful understanding of how God watches over us. He used the analogy of how grandparents watch over young grandchildren. I easily related because we had just spent a couple days caring for our year-old granddaughter while her parents took a weekend vacation.

How we watched over little Breanah during that time! We followed her around from room to room, never letting her out of our sight. Sometimes we held her hand. Sometimes we got in front of her for protection. Sometimes we picked her up and carried her when the path was too difficult or when she was too tired to walk. Sometimes we coaxed, "This way, Breanah. Come to Nana. Come to Papa. Come this way." And sometimes, too, we stayed out of sight, letting her explore, struggle, and learn. But even when she couldn't see us, we could always see her. Every moment we were close by. We were watching over her because we love her so much. And all the while we were watching, our thoughts of her were precious.

In a teeny-weeny way, our watch care of Breanah gives a glimpse of how God lovingly watches over us. We never have to wonder if He sees us. No matter what the storm, still He knows the way we take. He knows what's going on in our lives, in our hearts.

Whether we can see Him or not, God's voice still rises above the roar of every raging storm. With tenderness and strength He calls to us: *I know. I care. Always and forever, I am your hope and ever-present help in trouble.*

Ron Mehl was the kind of person that the better you knew him, the more you loved him. I am sure this story written by Ron will touch your heart as it has mine. When you come to the final sentence, of course the answer is yes!

He was a strong man facing an enemy beyond his strength.

His young wife had become gravely ill, then suddenly passed away, leaving the big man alone with a wide-eyed, flaxen-haired girl, not quite five years old.

The service in the village chapel was simple, and heavy with grief. After the burial at the small cemetery, the man's neighbors gathered around him. "Please, bring your little girl and stay with us for several days," someone said. "You shouldn't go back home just yet."

Brokenhearted though he was, the man answered, "Thank you, friends, for the kind offer. But we need to go back home—where she was. My baby and I must face this."

So they returned, the big man and his little girl, to what now seemed an empty, lifeless house. The man brought his daughter's little bed into his room, so they could face the first dark night together.

As the minutes slipped by that night, the young girl was having a dreadful time trying to sleep . . . and so was her father. What could pierce a man's heart deeper than a child sobbing for a mother who would never come back?

Long into the night the little one continued to weep. The big man reached down into her bed and tried to comfort her as best he could. After a while, the little girl managed to stop crying—but only out of sorrow for her father. Thinking his daughter was asleep, the father looked up and said brokenly, "I trust You, Father, but . . . it's as dark as midnight!"

Hearing her dad's prayer, the little girl began to cry again.

"I thought you were asleep, baby," he said.

"Papa, I did try. I was sorry for you. I did try. But—I couldn't go to sleep. Papa, did you ever know it could be so dark? Why, Papa? I can't even see you, it's so dark." Then, through her tears, the little girl whispered, "But you love me even if it's dark—don't you, Papa? You love me even if I don't see you, don't you, Papa?"

For an answer, the big man reached across with his massive hands, lifted his little girl out of her bed, brought her over onto his chest, and held her, until at last she fell asleep.

When she was finally quiet, he began to pray. He took his little daughter's cry to him, and passed it up to God.

"Father, it's dark as midnight. I can't see You at all. But You love me, even when it's dark and I can't see, don't You?"

RON MEHL
From *God Works the Night Shift* [6]

A Gentle Touch
For discussion or journaling

How precious also are Your thoughts to me, O God!
How great is the sum of them!
If I should count them, they would be more in number than the sand.

PSALM 139:17–18

1. Describe one of the times when you really felt God tenderly watching over you.
2. Write down a few sentences expressing what the verse at the top of this page means to you.
3. What is one of your favorite Bible verses that you turn to when you need a touch of hope? If you don't already have such a favorite, pick one from this chapter, write it on a card, and place that card in your purse or by your bedside.

A Prayer from the Heart

Dear Lord,

Thank You for being my refuge and strength when times of trouble come. You know what I'm facing today, and I pray that You will lift the fear from my heart and replace it with trust and peace. Your Word says that Your face is turned toward me and that You place Your hand of blessing on my head. Oh, Lord, I praise You for Your mercy and grace. Thank You for tenderly watching over those I love, and thank You for tenderly watching over me.

Chapter 2

PICTURE
OF PEACE

Jesus Christ is not a security from storms.
He is perfect security in storms.

KATHY TROCCOLI

It's a story my mother told to her grandchildren, and now I tell it to mine. It never seems to lose its charm, because the message is both timeless and powerful:

A noble king sent word to all his subjects that he would hold a contest to see who could paint the finest picture of peace. Many artists tried, and the king carefully studied each of their paintings. All were beautiful, but two were clearly outstanding.

One painting depicted a still, lone lake with tranquil mountains in the distance. In the foreground, pink and yellow flowers were scattered like confetti on a plush green meadow. Overhead the sun shone, and a few puffy white clouds drifted in a faultless blue sky.

The other artist had painted rugged mountains towering above a group of fragile birch trees bent down by blustery winds. Flashes of silver lightning streaked the darkening sky, and a turbulent waterfall thundered down the side of one of the mountains.

The king chose the second painting as the winner of the contest. Why? Because when he looked closely, the king saw something behind the waterfall. A scraggly bush grew out of a crevice, and at the fork of one of its branches a robin had built her nest. In the midst of the raging storm, with her head tucked serenely under her wing, the little bird was sound asleep.[1]

Isn't this the kind of peace we all desire—the ability to rest serenely even when storms rage all around us? That's exactly the kind of peace we can find in Jesus. Although He never promises us the absence of storms, He does promise His peace in the midst of them—and that peace is the essence of hope.

God Doesn't Say "If"

Remember the verse from the twenty-third chapter of Job that we looked at in the previous chapter?

> But He knows the way that I take;
> When He has tested me,
>   I shall come forth as gold.

Note that the second phrase of this verse begins, "When He has tested me." I wish it said "if" instead of "when," but it doesn't. Difficulties in life are simply a given.

Quite a few years ago now, an author named M. Scott Peck became famous for the opening phrase in his book *The Road Less Traveled*: "Life is difficult."[2] Although this was a startling way to open a book, the idea certainly wasn't original with Dr. Peck. In the Bible, the hardship of life is a reoccurring theme that begins in the third chapter of Genesis and runs all the way through the book of Revelation. Again and again God warns us that, because Adam and Eve chose to sin, life on earth will forever be filled with trouble. Chances are we will always be in the middle of some kind of difficulty—or just getting through it, or getting ready to face it. It's just part of our journey.

But, of course, there is a more treasured theme in the Bible—one that outshines every mention of inevitable trouble. Christ has won the victory. He is triumphant over all the heartaches of the world. Can't you hear His powerful voice echoing through the ages: "In the world you will have tribulation; but be of good cheer, I have overcome the world"?[3] That's why, even when storms rage, we can rest as serenely as the robin in the painting. We can have a peace that "surpasses all understanding."[4]

You probably know all that. But you've also probably discovered that simply *knowing* doesn't necessarily bring a sense of peace and hope when life gets difficult. Plenty of Christians, after all, still struggle with fear and despair. So do I at times. And so do you. What we need in times like those is something solid to grab on to when the stormy times come and we're feeling distinctly unpeaceful. Even in the most devastating times, I have found three dependable lifelines—three truths about peace and hope that have helped me not only keep my head above water, but also to find a heart of hope in the midst of it all.

First, the removal of the storm is not our peace. Jesus is our peace.

Second, the Lord stays with us during the storm.

Three, the closer we move to Him, the more peace we find.

He Is Our Peace

Last words are important. And it was on that final walk between the Upper Room and the Garden of Gethsemane, right before Jesus was arrested, tried, and crucified, that He spoke to His disciples about peace. Before Jesus prayed His last prayer for them, He first encouraged them in their faith and explained why He had to go away. He talked about the suffering and sorrow they would experience, and He never promised to make that suffering and sorrow go away. Instead, He assured them that He had already overcome the tribulation of the world. And even more important, He said, "These things I have spoken to you, that *in Me* you may have peace."[5]

Real, true, lasting peace, in other words, is found not in circumstances, but in a Person.

Jesus knew that in a matter of hours the victory song would be sung. His death on the cross and His bodily resurrection would be the final triumph over sin, suffering, and death. And it happened just as Jesus knew it would. He is the Overcomer. He is our Hope, the Eternal Ruler of the past, present, and future. The Lord of all.[6]

There is no one else. No place. No substance. Nothing on this earth can give us eternal peace. Only Jesus. Even though it is natural to want our troubles to go away, simply having them disappear will not bring us true peace. For that, we need Jesus.

> *Peace does not dwell in outward things, but in the heart prepared to wait trustfully and quietly on Him who has all things safely in His hands.*
>
> ELISABETH ELLIOT

Last week we experienced what is known in Arizona as a monsoon storm—and monsoon storms are something to see. The heavens open up in earnest over our usually arid part of the world. And during this recent storm, an occurrence with one of our granddaughters gave me a glimpse of an eternal truth.

Three-year-old Summer Malu was the first to notice black storm clouds gathering on the horizon. After showing them to us, she reached her arms up to Papa in a pick-me-up signal. Al gathered her up, and we just had time to rush inside before a sudden, fierce wind knocked over our patio chairs and torrents of rain poured down so fast that my husband was soaking wet in the few seconds it took to dash back outside and rescue the chairs. Then we all huddled near the living room windows and watched the storm rage.

Lightning flashed, thunder crashed, sirens wailed. And through it all, little Summer Malu clung to Al and was content. Not once did she ask him to make the storm go away. In her simple faith, all she wanted was to snuggle close to Papa.

That's exactly the kind of peace we experience when we trust Jesus. It doesn't come from having our problems vanish. It comes when we snuggle close to the One who truly is our peace.

The Lord Stays with Us

If we are to reach out to the One who is our peace and rest in His presence, we need to be absolutely certain He will be there when we need Him. That brings us to the second lifeline.

Remember in the last chapter we talked about how God knows where we are going and what happens to us? The promise that God actually stays with us in the midst of our troubles is even more intimate—more wonderful. And staying with us is one of God's unconditional promises, meaning that its fulfillment doesn't depend on anything we do or don't do. It just is. God repeats this promise over and over in Scripture. Here are just a few examples I've underlined in my Bible:

- "I have called you by your name; you are Mine. When you pass through the waters, I will be with you."

- "I am with you always . . . even to the end of the age."

- "Nothing in all creation will ever be able to separate us from the love of God that is revealed in Christ Jesus our Lord."

- "I will never leave you nor forsake you."[7]

I hope you don't mind if I share one more personal story—about an experience that helped me understand the power of these scriptural promises.

I'd been having frequent headaches, periodic dizziness, and recurring blurred vision for several months, so my doctor made an appointment for me to have an MRI. Because I'm a bit claustrophobic, I was more apprehensive about the procedure than I was about the possible outcome. My husband drove me to the appointment, and knowing he would stay with me during the procedure calmed me a little. When the nurse came to get me, however, she explained in a rather brusque tone that Al would have to stay in the waiting room. Al saw my panicked look and asked if there could be an exception. She was sorry, but no. So he squeezed my hand, promised to pray the whole time I was taking the test, and assured me that everything would be okay.

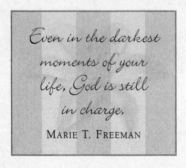

Even in the darkest moments of your life, God is still in charge.

MARIE T. FREEMAN

Well, as far as I was concerned, everything wasn't okay. By the time I walked into the examining room, my heart was fluttering like a frightened sparrow.

The cavernous room was empty except for an ugly, tunnel-shaped machine. Above the back wall were dark windows, and I couldn't see who or what was behind them. I couldn't even tell if the room was hot or cold, because sometimes I felt like shivering and other times there was damp perspiration, of all places, on my chin! (MRI procedures have improved a lot in the years since my procedure, so if you are ever scheduled for one, I'm sure the surroundings will be less intimidating.) The nurse, whose voice was now more patient than in the waiting room, carefully explained how the test worked. I would lie down on the bed of the tunnel machine for about twenty minutes. She would cover my eyes with a towel and then place a brace around my waist so I wouldn't move during the procedure. She said not to be frightened by loud knocking noises, because these were just a routine part of the test. She also said I would periodically hear other strange sounds—difficult to describe, but again, they were just a normal part of the test.

As the nurse was snapping the brace around me, she asked if I had any questions. (Although I didn't say so, I was thinking things like *What if I need to throw up?* or *What if I just rip off the brace and run out of here?*)

"Just one question," I finally answered. "In case something goes wrong, who will be with me during the test?" Her reply was so reassuring that even my sparrow's heart stopped fluttering.

"Don't worry," she said. "I will stay close by you the entire time. Even though you will not be able to see me, I will be able to see you. I won't leave. I will be here the entire time, making sure that you are okay."

You have no idea how reassuring that nurse's answer was. It makes a difference when someone stays with you during the storm. And that's what the King of kings promises He will do.

Isn't that absolutely astounding?

And doesn't it make you feel a little more hopeful, a little more at peace?

Press Closer to Him

Often the accumulation of desperate sorrows and everyday disappointments can tempt us to pull back from the Lord— but this is exactly when we need to draw closer to Him. For the third lifeline, I'd like to share six steps that have helped me stay close to God even when storms rage in my life. (I first wrote them in a book called *The Worn Out Woman*,[8] which I coauthored with a wonderful Christian psychologist named Steve Stephens.) To help me remember the steps, I use the acronym C-L-O-S-E-R.

C—Come. Jesus constantly invited people to come and spend time with Him. He wants to listen, to comfort, to help. Let His words connect with your longings: "Come to me, all of you who are weary and carry heavy burdens, and I will give you rest."[9]

L—Lean. When my mother, who paid her rent in life's heartbreak hotel, was going through an especially difficult time, I remember her saying, "I don't know where my Good Shepherd is taking me, but I'll keep leaning on Him all the way." The Lord is faithful and strong—good for leaning.

O—Open Your Bible. God wants His Word to be an oasis for your soul, and He has filled it with hope-filled verses that fit your heartbreak. The Psalms, especially, speak directly to our disappointments with words of comfort, but many other Scripture passages offer their own form of re-assurance and guidance.

S—Surrender. I sometimes doubt God because I don't think He is working things out my way or on my time schedule. Surrendering means trusting God's way and God's time schedule.

E—Eternalize. I remember times when I would discuss my disappointments with our friend and pastor, Loren Fischer. He would remove his glasses and lay them down on his desk and say, "We are seeing this through our viewpoint." Then, as he opened the Bible, he would deliberately pick up his glasses and, while putting them on, say, "Let's try and find God's perspective."

R—Release. Release means giving everything to God. It means packing up all the worry, all the what-ifs, all the doubts, all the debris from our shattered dreams, and giving them to Him.

This last point, I believe, is the most essential key to experiencing the Lord's peace in the midst of troubling circumstances. The more we can hand over what is bothering us to Him, the more peaceful our hearts will be.

But release isn't always easy to do. Sometimes it feels almost impossible. Because it is so hard to do, I often recommend this idea from Barbara Johnson, a gifted writer and speaker who has had many sorrows come crashing down around her. When it comes to releasing shattered dreams, Barbara suggests picturing in your mind that you are placing whatever breaks your heart into a gift box wrapped with lovely paper and ribbon. Then imagine walking into a glorious throne room where Jesus is waiting. Place the package in His arms and watch as He removes the wrapping and tenderly holds your gift close to His heart. Once assured that He will tenderly care for your worries and disappointments, leave them with Him. It's okay if you look over your shoulder now and then to make sure Jesus is still holding them. And, yes, He always is.

There are other ways to help your heart let go of your troubles, but I especially like Barbara's idea because it is a conscious way of moving closer to the One who will never let you go, who stays beside you in every difficulty and speaks peace to your heart.

Feel His heartbeat in the darkness, always there, closer than your closest friend.

Then nestle close, a little bird safe in the hands of a mighty God.

Spare Parts and Big Feet

Barbara Johnson says, "Laughter is the language of hope. We cry. We moan. We pray for help. And because we hold on to hope, we are eventually able to laugh again, even in the dark places." Barbara is best known as one of the original speakers with Women of Faith and for best-selling books such as Plant a Geranium in Your Cranium *and* Living Somewhere Between Estrogen and Death. *I know you will enjoy her winsome story about the circumstances in which she discovered the tiniest pin-prick of peaceful hope in the middle of a very big storm.*

Because of my battle with cancer, it's been a while since I've appeared onstage at a Women of Faith conference. If you've attended one in years gone by, however, I hope you remember me as presenting at least a marginally put-together appearance when I was a regular part of the speaker team: my hair combed, makeup camouflaging my wrinkles, and a colorful outfit helping me hide a few extra pounds under the spotlights. (Okay, so the buttons were probably held on with safety pins, and my usual "bracelet" was a bunch of rubber bands I'd picked up somewhere, but I always tried to look good—at least from a distance.)

If that's the image of me you remember, then you would have been shocked to have seen me during my first two years of recovery. Most of my hair was shaved off in the very first week of my cancer ordeal because I had to undergo brain surgery. And the hair that escaped the surgical scalping soon fell out due to the chemo. Other medication caused some swelling and weight gain, but I have to admit there was a pleasant sub-side effect to *that* side effect: My face rounded out into a nice, smooth ball that took out all my wrinkles!

I was managing to keep a pretty good attitude about the whole experience until, after the first round of chemo, I fell down and knocked out my front tooth!

Lord, I fumed at the Great Physician as I scowled into the mirror, *it's not enough that I'm bald and bloated, but I had to knock my tooth out too?!*

My dentist made me a temporary bridge, but he couldn't do a permanent repair until another health problem was resolved. So for more than a year I had to make sure all my spare parts were in place whenever I ventured outside my home. I had to check that both my wig and my fake tooth were on straight before I dared go out in public. I was afraid I'd see someone who'd known me in my former life and scare her into convulsions!

To make matters worse, my feet were chronically swollen. I complained to my doctor that all my shoes were too tight, hoping he might adjust my medication, but instead he told me, "Just buy bigger shoes!"

My pal Lynda heard about that directive and, always eager to help, showed up at my door bearing a little gift for me. Actually I should say she brought a *big* gift: her husband's size-thirteen house shoes! As if the slippers' size alone didn't make them large enough to fill my entire living room, they were shaped like moose heads—with antlers extending out to either side.

I wouldn't even think of wearing them—until Lynda insisted that I slip them on. I could have fit both feet *and* my arms up to my elbows inside them, so there was no question that they had plenty of capacity, no matter how big my feet planned to swell. It was impossible to walk in them; I could only shuffle. But for some strange reason, in the evenings when Bill and I were finished with the day's office work and doctor appointments, I would find myself settling back in my easy chair—my hair off and my tooth out—*wanting* to slip my feet into those ridiculous moose heads. They *were* warm and cozy, and there was another benefit: Just looking at them propped up on the footrest made me giggle.

It was in those private moments that the most unexpected sense of peace would sweep over me. I'd sit there thinking, *Here I am, still battling cancer, still sporting a hairstyle more appropriate for a marine than a grandmother, my front tooth out and my wig two rooms away—and yet I have an overwhelming feeling that all is well. As ridiculous as it might be to someone else, I feel like I'm in heaven on earth.*

The first time the attitude came over me, it was so surprising and so strong that I had to pause a moment to think about it, remembering Oscar Wilde's remark: "We are all in the gutter, but some of us are looking at the stars." That's exactly where I found myself. Looking out from a life that had been brutally kicked off course, I was still able to see God's gleaming promises of heavenly hope twinkling in the distance. And in those moments, I didn't worry about the medical procedures I faced or the gap in my smile or the beams of light bouncing off my bald head.

The tiniest pinprick of hope twinkling in our lives can restore us and empower us. As some wise person once said, human beings can live about forty days without food, about three days without water, about eight minutes without air . . . but only one second without hope. And that one little second of hope can work wonders.

BARBARA JOHNSON
From *Irrepressible Hope*[10]

A Gentle Touch
For discussion or journaling

He will shield you with his wings.
   He will shelter you with his feathers.
   His faithful promises are your armor and protection.

PSALM 91:4
NEW LIVING TRANSLATION

1. If you were an artist, what kind of picture would you paint to illustrate true, lasting peace?

2. Have you ever had to face a scary situation when you felt you were all alone? What was it like? If the storm lingered, how were you able to find even the "tiniest pinprick of hope"?

3. Choose one of the three lifelines mentioned in this chapter and describe how it might help when you face difficult times. First, the removal of the storm is not our peace. Jesus is our peace. Second, the Lord stays with us during the storm. Third, the closer we move to Him, the more peace we find.

A Prayer from the Heart

Dear Lord,

You are the shelter I run to when trouble rains down on my life. You touch my heart with words of comfort and fill my life with promises of hope. In times of sorrow and disappointment, teach me to press ever closer to You. You are the only One who can renew my weary spirit and provide me a sanctuary of peace. Thank You for blessing me so abundantly.

Chapter 3

SOMETHING
BEAUTIFUL

Like a lighthouse guiding those who are lost,
true hope shines on,
and even the blackest darkness
cannot overcome the power of its light.

KIM MILLER

Her name was Julia, and though I never actually met her, I have never forgotten her story. I learned it from her aunt in the little town called Sisters, Oregon, where my husband and I used to live.

Every year, in the early fall, women from all over the country gather in this charming mountain community for an event called Sisters in Sisters, which is best described as a celebration of family, friendship, and life. A few years ago, I was asked to give the closing keynote address for this gathering. And one afternoon when I was working on my speech, I received a call from an acquaintance of a friend of mine, who asked if we could get together for an hour or so. She wanted to tell me about her niece Julia, who had attended Sisters in Sisters the previous year. She hoped I could find a way to weave the story into my talk.

I had purchased fresh strawberries from a local fruit stand earlier that morning. While waiting for Julia's aunt to arrive, I quickly rinsed them, patted them dry, and just had time to arrange them on a pretty plate before the doorbell rang. After brief introductions, we took our coffee and strawberries into the living room and sank into the two most comfortable chairs, where she told me an amazing tale.

For most of her life, Julia was as unpleasant as she was beautiful and influential. She not only flaunted the fact that she was from a wealthy family and prominent in the community; she seemed to enjoy putting people in their place. Known for her volatile temper and her skill at inflicting verbal wounds, she cast off relationships as easily as a jacket on a muggy day but held on tightly to the smallest grudges. Not surprisingly, family members were often the recipients of her caustic remarks and temper flareups, so even these relationships were fragile at best.

What a sad life! That's what I was thinking as I listened to all this. Julia's aunt agreed, but the look on her face told me there was more to the story.

At first it looked like a turn for the worse. In her midforties, Julia was diagnosed with an aggressive form of cancer. She endured a series of uncomfortable treatments, but nothing stopped the progression of the disease. When she attended Sisters in Sisters, in fact, she had less than a year to live.

By that point, however, a remarkable change was taking place in Julia's life.

Shaken by her diagnosis, she had sought spiritual counsel for the first time in her life and had begun reading the New Testament. Shortly after accepting Jesus Christ as her Savior, she had felt a deep longing to seek forgiveness from those she had hurt. She wrote letters, made phone calls, invited people for coffee and apologies—did everything she could to restore relationships and create positive memories, especially with her family.

To her joy, many of her efforts were successful. She made peace with her ex-husband, grew close to her children, and developed a loving circle of Christian friends.

Several weeks before she died, Julia met with her pastor to discuss the final arrangements for her funeral. She told him she actually considered her cancer to be a love gift from God. As terrible as it was, she believed the Lord had used her tragedy to draw her to Himself. Julia's face was radiant when she told her pastor she would gladly exchange all her years of beauty, wealth, and influence for the two years of illness that taught her the unspeakable joy of loving Jesus and loving others.

To me, Julia's story is a striking illustration of Job 23:10, which we've been considering in the last few chapters:

> But He knows the way that I take;
> When He has tested me,
> I shall come forth as gold.

Isn't that exactly what happened to Julia? The Lord used the extremely trying circumstance of terminal cancer to change her life.

Though we all would prefer a life without severe difficulties, troubles come whether we like it or not. The good and hopeful news is that God often uses sorrow as a catalyst to make our lives truly beautiful.

"How would you like to have a friend who matures you, presses you closer to Jesus, and helps you have a powerful witness for the Lord?" asks nationally known pastor Adrian Rogers. Then he adds, "You have such a friend. Her name is Sorrow."[1]

Poet Robert Browning Hamilton put it another way.

> I walked a mile with Pleasure
> She chatted all the way
> But left me none the wiser
> For all she had to say.
>
> I walked a mile with Sorrow
> And ne'er a word said she;
> But oh, the things I learned from her
> When Sorrow walked with me![2]

But here's the problem: although we all get to know trouble and pain at some point in our lifetimes, not everyone comes out the wiser for it. Not everyone finds a way to make sorrow a friend. If we cannot trust that God is allowing the difficulties in our lives to make us better, it is all too likely that we will become bitter instead.

I believe that's one of the reasons God gave us the book of Job—to give us an example of how times of sorrow can help our lives to shine for Him. Although I still have questions about the whys of shattered dreams and broken lives, by reading the book of Job I've discovered some answers about how to respond when those dreaded times come.

Lessons from Job

To help me remember what I learned in Job about responding to sorrow, I divided the book into four scenes, like acts of a play where the props or characters change. From each scene I've tried to glean at least one truth I could live by. Here's a quick summary of what I found:

Scene One (Job 1:1)

The book of Job opens with a quick assessment of Job's character in the very first verse:

> There was a man in the land of Uz, whose name was Job; and that man was blameless and upright, and one who feared God and shunned evil.

Job, obviously, was a very good person. This doesn't mean he never sinned—only Christ can claim that distinction. But this verse makes it clear that Job's godliness was genuine and his moral character upright.

For me, this single verse destroys the notion that suffering is always the result of wrong choices—that while living on earth the righteous will always prosper and the wicked will always suffer. It is true that we bring many sorrows upon ourselves because we act foolishly or rebelliously, but not all heartbreaks are the result of our own sin.

What does this tell me about how to respond to trouble? It's certainly appropriate to examine my heart and repent for whatever I've done wrong and try to make amends to those I've hurt. That's part of the way God

> *Suffering may be someone's fault or it may not be anyone's fault. But if given to God, our suffering becomes an opportunity to experience the power of God at work in our lives and to give glory to Him.*
>
> ANNE GRAHAM LOTZ

wants us to live. But I also need to remember that God's purposes may be far different from anything I can see or understand. Over time, He may grant me glimpses of what He is doing in my life. Or I might never know the answers to why in my lifetime. But I can trust God to use the sorrows in my life to help me become truly beautiful in His eyes.

Scene Two (Job 1:2–22)

After Job learns that all his cattle, all his servants, and all his children have died, he makes an astounding statement in verses 20–21:

Then Job arose, tore his robe, and shaved his head; and he fell to the ground and worshiped.

And he said:

> "Naked I came from my mother's womb,
> And naked shall I return there.
> The LORD gave, and the LORD has taken away;
> Blessed be the name of the LORD."

Except for the words of our Lord Jesus, I think this is the most incredible response to suffering I have ever read. Job has just lost practically everything he cared about in this life. And still he falls to the ground, worships, and blesses God's name. Is it any wonder that for so many who suffer deeply, the worn pages of their Bible fall open to the book of Job?

Years ago, I remember hearing about the powerful message African-American pastor E. V. Hill preached at his wife's funeral. At the time, Dr. Hill had served for almost thirty years as pastor of Mt. Zion Missionary Church in the heart of the inner city of Los Angeles. He had received numerous awards and had even been honored by *Time* magazine as one of the seven most outstanding preachers in the twentieth century. From the beginning of his ministry, he had credited his wife, Jane, as being his greatest fan and encourager. Not surprisingly, her death was very difficult for Dr. Hill. He admitted that on the way to the memorial service he still had no idea of what he would say.

Even though his shoulders were bent with grief, Dr. Hill was an imposing figure as he walked to the platform. Looking out at the huge gathering of friends who had come to honor his wife, Dr. Hill felt the power of the Holy Spirit surge through him. In a strong yet worshipful voice, the first words he spoke were: "The LORD gave, and the LORD hath taken away; blessed be the name of the LORD."[3]

Like Job, in the middle of a great sorrow, Dr. Hill worshiped and praised the Lord. How I desire for this to be my own response to the heartbreaks of life. This morning, in fact, I asked the Lord's forgiveness for the complaining way I usually react even when small disappointments come my way—let alone the big heartaches. I want to have a heart that trusts God no matter what. Beginning this morning, and I hope for many other mornings to follow, I'm determined to spend more time in worship and praise, even when—and especially when— things are going wrong in my life.

> One morning I awoke earlier than usual with the dawn just breaking over the mountains. Suddenly, I realized a symphony of bird songs was literally surrounding me. The air was liquid with music, as if the whole creation were praising God at the beginning of a new day. . . . And I learned a lesson. I had been beginning my days with petitions, and I should have been beginning them with praise.
>
> RUTH BELL GRAHAM

Scene Three (Job 2:1–37:24)

The next "scene" from Job is really a series of small scenes, and it takes up most of the book of Job. These thirty-some chapters feature an ongoing argument between Job and his "friends" about why God allowed or caused Job's suffering. At one point, Job calls these other men "miserable comforters"[4] because they seem more bent on agitating him than giving understanding and solace. (Perhaps this is a good lesson on how not to comfort others.)

But there is another theme I want to highlight in this long scene. Job begins asking God questions, the same kind of questions we might want to ask if we were hoping for a face-to-face meeting with God during a time of sorrow—questions like these:

- Why did You let this happen?

- What have I done to deserve this?

- How long before You bless me again?

Even though I want to remember the lesson of praise and worship from scene two, there is a balancing truth I need to understand, which is that I can be honest with God about my hopes and my fears and my questions.

This concept of expressing our honest feelings to God is something my friend Barbara Baumgardner encourages when she gives seminars on keeping a spiritual journal. She suggests that when we are writing our thoughts to God, perhaps we should write about when we are morbidly sad or fiercely angry as well as when we are incredibly happy. Then Barbara adds with a smile, "It's okay. God can handle our honesty. He knows anyway."

Oh dear. I've just reread what I have written in the last few paragraphs, and I'm getting a little nudge to my heart to add that healthy honesty with God must also include a deep respect for who God is. Evidently Job held on to that sense of respect, because on two different occasions the book of Job records that he did not sin while expressing his feelings.[5] Let's keep that in mind as we move on to the last scene, where we see how God responded to Job's questions.

Scene Four (Job 38:1–42:17)

The curtain goes up on chapter 38 with these words: "Then the LORD answered Job out of the whirlwind."

Wow! That is so incredibly wonderful—another reminder that God was there all the time and knew all about what Job and his friends had been discussing.

After thirty-some chapters of speculation about what God is doing in Job's life, God finally gives some direct answers. These answers are very different from what Job expected, however. Instead of explaining His ways and His reasons, God showed Job glimpses of His majesty, power, knowledge, wisdom, and authority.

In the Scofield Bible, the explanatory note for chapter 42 reminds us that "beyond the revealed purposes of God there still remains much of mystery. And for this there is no answer except the attitude of worship in which we humbly acknowledge that a sovereign God cannot be required . . . to give all the reasons for what He chooses to do."[6]

Don't you think that it blesses God when we trust Him just because of who He is? Certainly, as God reminded Job, we can see His attributes in creation, and they are altogether good. And how can we think of the cross of Calvary and not trust His heart?

I hope you will take time to read the entirety of God's response in chapters 38 through 42 of the book of Job. I find these passages so precious that it is my habit to read them out loud, all the way through, on the first day of every year. After meditating on God's majesty, I commit my days, my dreams, and my plans for the year to the One whose name is above all else.

The Finale

As the final curtain falls on the book of Job, we see God blessing Job twofold for all he had lost. We learn that Job lived long enough to have seven more children and many grandchildren. The last words in the book of Job tell us that he "died, old and full of days."[7]

Could God have protected Job from his heartaches and sorrows?

Absolutely.

Can He protect us from heartaches and sorrows?

Absolutely.

But instead He will allow and, yes, even plan storms for our lives. Why? Because He has purposes too wonderful for us to understand. Our part in the whole scenario is to examine our hearts and to trust and worship and praise in such a way that when we are tested we will indeed come forth as gold.

The Gold Refiner

Although it is familiar, the story of the gold refiner must be told here so I can properly conclude these chapters on Job. (Besides, as you know, I love stories!) Perhaps you can pretend you haven't read it before or at least try to read it with new eyes.

A woman visited a gold refiner's shop and watched as he placed a large cauldron over the fire. The cauldron was filled with a dark fluid, and the gold refiner constantly checked the temperature as he watched and stirred the bubbling liquid. Periodically he carefully skimmed off the impurities that rose to the top and discarded them.

At one point, the woman asked, "Sir, do you always watch so closely while the work of the refining is going on?"

"Oh, yes," he replied. "I must keep my eye steadily fixed on the fire, for if the time needed for refining is exceeded or if the fire becomes too hot, the gold can be damaged beyond repair."

His answer caused her to think about the sorrow that she was going through, and she found comfort in the thought that this is how it is with the Lord. When He allows His children to go through heartbreak, His eye is steadily intent on the process. He stands by at every moment, keeping a close watch.

Just as the woman was about to leave, the gold refiner asked if she would like to know when the refining process was finished.

"Oh, yes," she answered.

With a gentle smile on his rugged face, the refiner answered, "The process is complete when I can see my own face reflected in the gold."

And so it is with us. When Christ sees His face reflected in us . . . we, too, will have come forth as gold.

A New Perspective

This story is by world-renowned evangelist Dr. Billy Graham. I just realized that in this chapter I've also included quotes by his wife and daughter—a family affair without even planning it. How fun! Dr. Graham's story is short, but the message is powerful.

I have a friend who lost his job, a fortune, a wife, and a home. But he tenaciously held to his faith—the only thing he had left. One day he stopped to watch some men doing stonework on a huge church. One of them was chiseling a triangular piece of stone.

"What are you going to do with that?" asked my friend. The workman said, "See that little opening way up there near the spire? Well, I'm shaping this down here, so it will fit up there."

Tears filled the eyes of my friend as he walked away, for it seemed that God had spoken through the workman to explain the ordeal through which he was passing. "I'm shaping you down here, so you'll fit in up there."

DR. BILLY GRAHAM
From *The Secret of Happiness* [8]

A Gentle Touch
For discussion or journaling

He has made everything beautiful in its time. Also He has put eternity in their hearts, except that no one can find out the work that God does from beginning to end.

ECCLESIASTES 3:11

1. Describe your feelings about the idea that God allows and, yes, even plans difficulties for our lives. How does your understanding affect your ability to hope?

2. How do you usually respond when heartbreaks crash down on you or those you love?

3. Find a time when you can carefully read out loud Job 38–42 and then write down a few thoughts about what you can know about God from these chapters.

A Prayer from the Heart

Dear Lord,

Please help me to become faithful in offering You praise and thanksgiving at the beginning and ending of each day—no matter what is going on in my life. I desire to know You more intimately than I ever have before—not only that You are awesome and majestic, but also that You are merciful and loving. Oh, dear Lord, I want to be beautiful in Your eyes.

Chapter 4

BLESSINGS

The soul would have no rainbow
had the eyes no tears.

AUTHOR UNKNOWN

Recently painted walls of honeysuckle yellow and a stenciled border of pink and blue handprints near the ceiling brightened the hospital room, a cheery contrast to the plain beige hallways. Although a cotton curtain was drawn halfway around the other bed, Mark and Susan were alone as they waited for the nurse to bring their newborn son for his first feeding.

A deep sigh of contentment escaped Susan's lips as she looked at her husband. *So handsome*, she thought. Even though he was a good preacher, Susan often wondered if his good looks were part of the reason the congregation had been so eager to have him as their new pastor. Squeezing her husband's hand, Susan glanced at the nightstand, where a single yellow rosebud graced a small white vase. The card propped up against the vase bore Mark's handwriting: "Welcome home, Danny. We love you. Mommy and Daddy." Susan had already decided she would press the rosebud, tie a blue ribbon around it, and place it with the card on the first page of Danny's baby book.

Mark and Susan were surprised and a little worried when Dr. Andersen came in instead of the nurse. "Is anything wrong?" Susan asked. Before answering, Dr. Andersen pulled a chair over close to them and sat down. "I'm sorry," he said softly. "But our preliminary findings indicate that Danny has Down syndrome." Dr. Andersen gave what information he thought Mark and Susan needed right away and then promised to come back in a few hours. Knowing they needed time alone, he closed the door as he left.

Wrapping their arms around each other, Mark and Susan struggled to comprehend what the doctor had told them. Giant tears dampened the bed covers, and their shoulders heaved as they cried deep sobs for their little Danny . . . mourning the loss of so many of their dreams for him and asking God all the unanswerable questions. The afternoon turned to evening, and it seemed they had cried a lifetime of tears before there was a gradual change in Mark and Susan's conversation. Like a flickering candle that somehow manages to stay lit in the wind, hope began to glimmer.

Susan was the first to say that she knew that God would help them through this. Surely nothing could come into their lives—or into little Danny's life—that the Lord did not allow or plan. She talked about another child they knew, a girl about eleven years old, who had Down syndrome. They remembered how happy she always seemed, looking at life with such pure innocence. Little Rachel loved helping people, and she loved Jesus with all her heart.

Mark whispered comforting words while Susan blew her nose and dabbed at the tears that still slid silently down her cheeks. They talked about what the future might bring and how they would tell others about their Danny. Finally, they were able to bow their heads and hearts before the Lord, thanking Him for their baby and asking for His guidance to be the very best parents Danny could ever have.

They heard a soft knock before the door opened. Turning, they saw a nurse holding Danny securely bundled in mounds of blue flannel. Susan eagerly reached for her son. Snuggling him close, she lifted a corner of the blanket and traced his face with her finger. A smile lifted her tear-stained cheeks as Susan looked up at the nurse. With love that only new mothers understand, Susan said, "Isn't he a precious baby!"

The nurse quickly agreed that indeed Danny was precious, but a momentary look of concern shadowed her kind face. Susan noticed her hesitation and quickly added, "God has chosen to bless us with a Down syndrome baby."

Is Danny a blessing? A thousand times yes, Mark and Susan would say, and they could give you a thousand reasons why. One of the specific moments of blessings they like to share is what happened the next Sunday at church. The nurse who brought Danny to their room had told the other nurses how Susan responded when she first held Danny, and the story quickly spread through their small Midwestern community. The following Sunday, many from the hospital staff and others from around town came to church to show their support for the young pastor and his wife. They also wanted to know more about the God whom Mark and Susan trusted so completely. When Mark gave the invitation to receive Christ as Savior, nine people responded. This was just the beginning of the blessings little Danny brought into the world.[1]

> *I discovered that sorrow was not to be feared but rather endured with hope and expectancy that God would use it to bless my life.*
>
> JILL BRISCOE

Looking for Blessings

It's one thing to count your blessings when life is sunny. It's quite another thing to look trouble in the face and look for a smile of blessing when storms crash on the shores of your happiness. Some people, like Mark and Susan, seem to do this almost instinctively. Their confidence in God's goodness and in His sovereign control is not shaken when storms descend, so they move quickly to a place of trust and hope. I, on the other hand, am the sort who usually needs time to wade through the deepest mud puddles before I start looking for a rainbow.

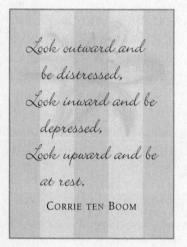

Look outward and be distressed,
Look inward and be depressed,
Look upward and be at rest.

CORRIE TEN BOOM

What can people like me do to get out of the puddles more quickly? As mentioned in the last chapter, it helps to put more of an emphasis on praise and worship in my daily life. Habits like pressing closer to the Lord and replacing worry with peace are important. But when I think of Mark and Susan, Julia near the end of her life, and Dr. E. V. Hill, I can see another quality they all seemed to share.

These people, as far as I can see, found blessings because they developed a different way of looking at what was happening in their lives. Instead of focusing only on those things they desired in the here and now—constant good health, plans succeeding, financial dreams coming true, someone to cherish us—they were able to keep their focus on eternal benefits.

The apostle Paul emphasized this long view when he was encouraging the church at Corinth during their struggles:

For our light affliction, which is but for a moment, is working for us a far more exceeding and eternal weight of glory,
while we do not look at the things which are seen, but at the
things which are not seen. For the things which are seen are
temporary, but the things which are not seen are eternal.[2]

If tears have taken up long-term residence in your heart, it
would be insensitive if I were to suggest that your affliction is
light or that your suffering is trivial. But Paul said exactly that
to the Corinthians. Perhaps the words didn't sound so harsh
coming from him because the people he was writing to knew
Paul had suffered so much—starvation, beatings, imprison-
ment, and a disability that the Lord did not heal. We know from
elsewhere in his letters that Paul felt all this suffering deeply and
cared about the suffering of others. So I believe he only uses
"light affliction" here for the purpose of contrast. He's saying
that even the most terrible and lingering kind of suffering on
earth will diminish if we view it from the perspective of eternity.

That's exactly the perspective that has helped me find
God's blessings in the midst of suffering. So I don't question
Paul's words, though I can't quite bring myself to say them
outright to someone who is hurting. (Good thing I can let
the Bible do the talking!) And I feel quite comfortable repeat-
ing to you, even if your heart is breaking, the essence of what
Paul wrote: real hope and true blessings come from what is
eternal, not what is temporary.

Here's an idea I tried that you might find helpful in finding
that kind of perspective for yourself. I made a list of everything
I could think of that is eternal or unchanging: heaven, God's
Word, God's attributes, Christ's love, our deeds that survive the
test of His refining fire, and eternal life. (Maybe you can think
of other things to add.) Once I had that list, I could easily see

that everything else I value and worry about, that I spend time and energy on, belonged on my list of temporary things.

For instance, no matter how much I exercise or how much healthy food I eat, my earthly body is temporary. No matter how many times I remodel, upgrade, paint, or decorate, my house is temporary. No matter how hard I work or how well I budget, my bank account is temporary. Everything I learned in school will eventually be lost. Even the relationships I value most will be temporary if my precious loved ones do not know Christ as Savior.

Improving Our Perspective

It's hard to hang on to that eternal perspective while trying to live here on earth. We naturally get distracted by thoughts and feelings and needs, by things that happen to us and things that happen within us. But if we can keep our focus on what lasts forever rather than on what is temporary, perhaps we will discover the secret of finding blessings even when life takes the most terrible turns.

If you're having a hard time developing such eternal eyesight, perhaps these few suggestions will help:

- Come to God honestly with your pain. Try to open your heart to what God is trying to do in your life.

- Ask Christian friends to pray for you in this time of difficulty—and to pray specifically for the gift of a different perspective.

- Consciously put aside your natural questions of "Why?" and "Why me?" Concentrate instead on receiving God's gift of comfort and strength so you will have the energy to look beyond.

- Seek out hopeful people to spend time with—not superficial, "perky" types, but those with a deeply positive, trusting attitude.

- Try to remember times in your life or the lives of people you've known when unwelcome events eventually brought blessing. Ask friends and family for examples too, or read some good inspirational stories. (Don't forget biblical ones.)

- Lean on the reality that if God has blessed others through adversity, He can do it for you as well.

- Spend as much time as possible in the Psalms, which can help train your heart and mind to journey more easily from pain to hope and trust in God's eternal goodness.

- Write out Romans 8:28–29 by hand and post it on your bathroom mirror to read with every visit. Keep reminding yourself that *nothing* can separate you from Christ's love.

The Blessing of Eternal Eyesight

Dr. Howard Hendricks is a well-known author and beloved professor at Dallas Theological Seminary. Al and I always try to take every opportunity to hear him preach, even if it means traveling a bit, because we know his messages are life-changing. One particularly memorable message of his concerned a visit he had made to one of the "leprosy centers" established in India under the guidance of Mother Teresa.

On the morning when Dr. Hendricks visited, they were having a praise service—not prayer, but praise! And near the close of the service, one of the women who had leprosy (Hansen's disease) hobbled to the platform. Hendricks said that even though she was partially blind and her face and body badly disfigured, she was one of the most beautiful women he had ever met.

Raising both of her nearly fingerless hands toward heaven, she said in a clear voice, "I want to praise God that I am a leper because it was through my leprosy that I came to know Jesus Christ as my Savior. And I would rather be a leper who knows Christ than be completely whole and a stranger to His grace."

This dear woman understood the difference between what is temporary and what is eternal. She had found the blessing.

Bedtime Blessings

*I first discovered the writings of Nancy Jo Sullivan when I was
doing research for a collection called* Stories for the Heart. *Her
stories were always among my favorites and invariably touched
my heart. Nancy and I first became friends by phone, and then I
had the privilege of working with her as a coeditor on several
story books. I wanted to end this chapter with something sweet
and inspirational. That's when I remembered this lovely story of
Nancy's, which never fails to bring hopeful tears to my eyes.*

I had a bad cold that evening, and I crawled into bed much earlier
than usual. While my husband and kids watched a movie down-
stairs, I huddled under blankets, my body achy and chilled. A soft
rain shower fell outside my bedroom window. I started to relax.
The sound of the dropping rain had a soothing rhythm, a soft, pat-
tering cadence that calmed me like a lullaby.

Just as I began drifting off to sleep, I noticed Sarah, my Down syndrome daughter, standing in the doorway. With her curly hair pulled
into pigtails, she was wearing a long robe and fluffy pink slippers.
Her petite silhouette was shadowed by a light in the hallway.

"Mom . . . you . . . you . . . forgot to tuck me in," she stuttered
in a respectful whisper.

For Sarah, daily patterns and routines were very important.
Even though she was sixteen years old, she still functioned at the
level of a first grader. I knew this family ritual that we called "tuck-

in-time" brought closure to her day and predictability to her life.

"Let's wait a while," I suggested as I motioned Sarah near. Without making a sound, Sarah sat down on the edge of my bed. For a moment, the two of us listened to the rain drumming on the roof above us.

"The rrrain is nnice," Sarah said.

I took her hand in mine. "It is," I replied as I began remembering her early childhood and the many mother-daughter moments I had spent at her bedside. Night after night, I had tucked her in, snuggling a quilt over her shoulders and tracing a small cross on her forehead.

I remembered one night when Sarah was about nine years old. I decided it was time to teach her a bedtime prayer. While Sarah nestled beneath her blankets, surrounded by pink-checked pillows and stuffed animals, I slowly repeated a rhyming passage about God and guardian angels, a simple four-line prayer.

"It's . . . It's . . .ttoo hhard ffor me," Sarah admitted with a sigh of dismay.

Stroking her hair, I saw her brow wrinkle with frustration.

"Sarah, what do you want to tell God?" I asked as I gently folded her small fingers into a clasp of prayer.

Sarah closed her eyes tightly as if formulating her thoughts.

"Dear God . . . I . . . I . . . love . . . mmy mom," she said.

Throughout the years, Sarah had offered this "mom-prayer" time and time again. Though she had never learned to memorize other childhood prayers, I had grown used to this nightly routine of guiding her through simple question-answer petitions.

But now, much to my surprise, I felt Sarah tug my bedspread over my shoulders, gently and tenderly smoothing each crease of the quilt.

"Mom, what ddo you wwant to tell God?" she asked as she traced a small cross on my forehead.

I closed my eyes. I felt like an adored child. I felt safe and secure. "Dear God . . . I love Sarah," I said softly.

Sarah smiled. The prayer lingered. The rain continued to fall in song-like beats, covering our home and sliding down my bedroom window in small streams. So, too, a shower of love was raining down on us from heaven, blessing us.

I began to doze as Sarah quietly tiptoed to her room across the hall. I heard the squeak of her box spring and the rumpling of covers as she crawled into bed. I wondered if I should help her settle in for the night. She's growing up . . . let her go, an inner voice whispered in my heart.

Curling up in the comfort and warmth of my bed, I called out to her. "Sarah, are you an angel?" I heard her giggling. She thought I was joking.

From across the hall she called back. "I . . . I . . . am." And the rain kept falling.

NANCY JO SULLIVAN
From *Stories for a Woman's Heart* [3]

A Gentle Touch
For discussion or journaling

Now may the God of hope fill you with all joy and peace in believing, that you may abound in hope by the power of the Holy Spirit.

ROMANS 15:13

1. What are some of the blessings you discovered during a time in your life that was especially difficult for you? (If you can't think of any, ask a friend for such an example from his or her life.)

2. Review the suggestions on pages 54–55 about developing eternal eyesight. Is there anything you would add to this list? On a daily basis, what on this list do you find the hardest to do? What is the easiest?

3. Try starting a gratitude journal. Every day for at least a week, write down three things that you are thankful for. You might want to involve the whole family and use it as a mealtime discussion. Or you might read through your list of blessings right before you fall asleep each night.

A Prayer from the Heart

Dear Lord,

Sometimes this idea of finding blessings in difficult times seems almost too hard, and yet I realize it is a key to finding peace and hope. Today I lift up open hands and open heart, inviting You to come in and nurture me. Teach me to look beyond the muddy puddles to the rainbow of Your promises.

Chapter 5

HUSH,
MY HEART

Fear not tomorrow,
for God is already there.

AUTHOR UNKNOWN

Have you ever had a night when no matter what you try, you just can't get to sleep? That's what was going on with my friend Heather—except it wasn't just one night. For two weeks straight she had tried all the conventional tips for getting a good night's rest but continued to have trouble falling asleep. Then, in spite of the fact that she was exhausted, she would wake up about three every morning and toss and turn until daylight.

She knew what the problem was. Heather said she had fallen into a hole of worry and she couldn't climb out.

Ron, her husband, had been laid off from work for almost seven months. He had worked a few temporary jobs in that time, but Heather worried that if something permanent didn't turn up soon, they could lose their home. A bigger worry was that she and Ron could no longer pay for their health insurance. The idea that one of her kids would get injured or come down with some awful illness kept running around in her mind, especially at night. On the rare times when she managed to give the house and insurance worries to the Lord, a new bunch of what-ifs jumped on the merry-go-round.

I knew about Heather's sleep problems. So I was pleasantly surprised when she called me one evening with her voice sounding kind of perky. She had come up with an idea and wanted to know if I could help.

Earlier that day, Heather had heard about a research project that intrigued her. The researchers concluded that more than 90 percent of the things people worry about are either events they regret in the past, present events they have no control over, or future events that will probably never happen. The other 10 percent, according to the researchers, can usually be resolved if people stop stewing and start doing something about them.

Heather's idea was to write her worries on paper and then try to put them in categories similar to the four mentioned in the research project—past regrets, uncontrollable events, unlikely futures, and solvable problems. She thought it would be good to get another person's perspective on her lists and wanted to know if I could come over the next afternoon before the kids got home from school. I thought it was a great idea and, yes, I could come.

Even with this plan settled, Heather's mind was still racing as we talked that night, and she wasn't sure if she could ramp down enough to fall asleep. I was about to offer to talk a while longer, but the Lord seemed to say to me, *It's all right. You can hang up now. I will rock Heather to sleep.* Of course I didn't hear an audible voice, but there was something so sweet about the thought that I just knew it came from the Lord.

Before saying good-bye, we quietly prayed together—spending most of the time thanking the Lord for His mercy and grace and lovingkindness and every other good thing we could think of. At the very end I prayed

A weary Christian lay awake one night trying to hold the world together by his worrying. Then he heard the Lord gently say, "You can go to sleep now, I'll sit up."

RUTH BELL GRAHAM

that the Lord would indeed hold Heather in His arms and rock her to sleep—that He would whisper words of hope and hush her heart.

I don't know whether Heather actually slept better that night. She never told me. I do know that *I* slept better, confident that my friend was safe in our Father's arms and that in the coming days He'd help her learn to handle her worry.

Worry Remedies

Worry can seem harmless, but actually it is one of Satan's most effective methods of attacking and critically wounding Christians. One reason worry can be so dangerous is that it tends to feed on itself—the more we worry, the more we worry. More important, when left unattended, worry can weaken our faith and even destroy our hope.

What's the alternative? Heather learned a lot about that in the four more months that passed before Ron's employer was able to hire him back. Although they didn't lose their home or face catastrophic medical bills, those months were pretty shaky for their little family. And yet Heather was able to get a handle on her worry. Here are some of the strategies that she learned.

Talking It Out

At first worry doesn't seem like such a bad thing—especially if it is just a way to express our concern about a problem so that we will be motivated to take action. However, once worry turns into a continual rehearsal of what might go wrong without any plan of action, then talking the situation out with someone else can help stop the cycle. There's a lot of truth in that old saying that sometimes we can't see the forest for the trees. It helps to step back and get perspective from someone else.

Of course, talking things out with the Lord is the first priority. We need to share our worries directly with the only One who can truly handle them. When Heather and I ended our telephone conversation with prayer, that's what we were doing—intentionally applying the remedy that God prescribes in Philippians 4:4–7:

> Rejoice in the Lord always. Again I will say, rejoice! Let your gentleness be known to all men. The Lord is at hand. Be anxious for nothing, but in everything by prayer and supplication, with thanksgiving, let your requests be made known to God; and the peace of God, which surpasses all understanding, will guard your hearts and minds through Christ Jesus.

Note that this verse stresses the importance of praying with joy and thanksgiving, even as we bring our worries to God. It doesn't say we are to be thankful *for* every situation, however. It just indicates that *in* every situation we can still find ways to wrap our requests with thanksgiving.

After talking things out with God, however, talking things over with another person—preferably someone who is mature in faith and encouraging by nature—is a practical follow-up. Your pastor or a counselor is an obvious choice, but a loving friend can sometimes be just as helpful.

Heather's plan to write her worries on paper and then brainstorm with me was a way to talk them out—get them out of her head so she could look at them more objectively. Once she did that, she could decide to act on whatever she could and turn the rest of the problems over to God.

It worked! By the time we finished that afternoon, Heather

had several fresh ideas to share with Ron. Her spirits had brightened considerably.

Working It Out

Just as muscles weaken when they aren't used, faith also gets wimpy when not used on a consistent basis. And wimpy faith doesn't have the spiritual vigor needed to fight off worry, especially when our world caves in. Since the object of our faith must be the Lord, not people or circumstances, sometimes making a change in our daily devotional routine can make a significant difference in building spiritual muscles.

Heather, for instance, was well grounded in the Word, but the circumstances of the last few months had left her exhausted and spiritually dry. She still faithfully kept up her morning devotions, following a schedule for reading the Bible through in a year. The only problem was that she was doing it out of habit rather than desire. She was missing the joy, hope, and encouragement that her routine had given her in the past, and now the words didn't seem to be sinking in. She didn't feel like anything she read was reaching the place where worry had taken up residence.

Although following a scheduled plan for reading Scripture is a wonderful idea, sometimes the pace can be too fast. When a person is under a lot of stress, or even if not, it might be better to intentionally take two years instead of one when reading the Bible through on a reading schedule. And to tell the truth—I'm really going to meddle here—when I'm hurting, I am rarely blessed by Leviticus, Numbers, or Deuteronomy. I need the comfort of the Psalms, the solace of Job, the hope of the Prophets, or the promises of the New Testament.

Heather decided to "give herself permission" to set aside

her scheduled reading for a while and concentrate instead on segments of Scripture that she loved or that were especially comforting. She also spent some time rereading journals she had written years before and was so inspired that she bought a brand-new one and started journaling again—another form of "talking it out" with God and her own heart.

Heather also selected a few passages to meditate on right before going to bed. Sometimes she would turn verses into prayers by inserting her name or the name of someone else she was concerned about. Other times, she simply wrote out entire passages in her journal.

There's nothing magical about these ideas, but when hard times come, they will help you realize that God is speaking directly to you through His Word. Often the knots of worry will start coming untangled and your faith will be strengthened.

Ten Suggested Scriptures for Meditation

Psalm 40
Psalm 91
Psalm 103
Isaiah 40:28-31
Jeremiah 29:11-14
Matthew 6:25-34
Matthew 11:28-30
Romans 8:35-39
Philippians 4:6-9
1 Peter 5:6-11

In his much-acclaimed book, *The Purpose Driven Life*, Rick Warren makes a thought-provoking comment about Scripture meditation:

When you think about a problem over and over in your mind, that's called worry. When you think about God's Word over and over in your mind, that's meditation. If you know how to worry, you already know how to meditate! You just need to switch your attention from your problems to Bible verses. The more you meditate on God's Word, the less you will have to worry about.[1]

Kind of puts things in perspective, doesn't it?

Waiting It Out

Thinking back to the night when Heather first called me about her worry, I can understand why her heart was so anxious. It was the waiting that wore her down. She felt that God had not only allowed something bad to happen to her and her family, but was taking far too long to fix it. She wanted her prayers answered now, but instead, God's answer was to wait and wait and wait.

God's waiting room is one of the most difficult places any of us can live. Waiting for a job to open. Waiting for a prodigal to come home. Waiting for an illness to run its course. Waiting for a broken relationship to mend. Waiting for . . .

And yet sometimes that is what God asks us to do. Do whatever you can to address the situation, and then . . . "Hang on. Don't give up. Wait it out. Trust Me."

The truth is, sometimes we have no choice but to wait. We can't control the progression of days or their events. But we do have a choice in *how* we wait. We can choose to spend the time in worry or anger—harming our health, our relationships, and even our faith. Or we can choose to hand our concerns over to the Lord and let Him take care of them. Even if God never "fixes" the situation the way we want or if we don't see the final outcome during our lifetime, we can still find peace and hope when we choose to trust Him.

During Heather's darkest days of worry, one of the verses that seemed to comfort her the most was Romans 15:4:

> For everything that was written in the past was written to teach us, so that through endurance and the encouragement of the Scriptures we might have hope.[2]

This is a wonderful verse. No wonder it brought Heather so much comfort. God is so dearly concerned about us, He recorded specific circumstances in the Bible that we can read and be encouraged and have hope. He longs for us to trust Him because He knows that trust is a healing balm for worry.

I once read about an unusual form of Chinese theater. With hand puppets, a play is acted out on two levels at the same time. The lower level shows the characters as they progress through the plot with terrible trials and tribulations. But on the upper level, the audience can see how the play will end . . . the villains are punished and the heroes rewarded. Evil loses. Good wins.

Because the audience can see the outcome by looking up, they are not overly worried when the situation looks hopeless. Instead, the audience begins to shout encouragement to the harried characters on the lower level. "Don't quit," they shout. "Don't give up!"

Don't you think that's what God is asking us to do? No matter how gloomy the present may seem, look up. God's Word promises that in the end, all will turn out well. He will provide. He will deliver. Good will win.

And yes, He will comfort our anxious hearts.

The Sparrow at Starbucks

In 1905, evangelist Dr. Walter S. Martin and his wife, Civilla, were in Elmira, New York, visiting friends by the name of Mr. and Mrs. Doolittle. Mrs. Doolittle had been bedridden for nearly twenty years, and her husband was so crippled that he could get around only with a wheelchair. In spite of these difficulties, the Doolittles were a constant source of inspiration and comfort to others. When Dr. Martin commented on their bright hopefulness and asked about its source, Mrs. Doolittle replied with a phrase based on Matthew 10:29–30: "His eye is on the sparrow, and I know He watches me." The beauty of her simple answer is what inspired Civilla Martin to write the lyrics of the beloved hymn "His Eye Is on the Sparrow."[3] As you will see in the following story, this song still brings inspiration and comfort a century later.

It was chilly in Manhattan but warm inside the Starbucks shop on 51st Street and Broadway, just a skip up from Times Square. Early November weather in New York City holds only the slightest hint of the bitter chill of late December and January, but it's enough to send the masses crowding indoors to vie for available space and warmth.

For a musician, it's the most lucrative Starbucks location in the world, I'm told, and consequently, the tips can be substantial if you play your tunes right. Apparently, we were striking all the right chords that night, because our basket was almost overflowing.

It was a fun, low-pressure gig—I was playing keyboard and singing backup for my friend who also added rhythm with an arsenal of percussion instruments. We mostly did pop songs from the '40s to the '90s with a few original tunes thrown in. During our emotional rendition of the classic, "If You Don't Know Me by Now," I noticed a lady sitting in one of the lounge chairs across from me. She was swaying to the beat and singing along.

After the tune was over, she approached me. "I apologize for singing along on that song. Did it bother you?" she asked.

"No," I replied. "We love it when the audience joins in. Would you like to sing up front on the next selection?"

To my delight, she accepted my invitation.

"You choose," I said. "What are you in the mood to sing?"

"Well . . . do you know any hymns?"

Hymns? This woman didn't know who she was dealing with. I cut my teeth on hymns. Before I was even born, I was going to church. I gave our guest singer a knowing look. "Name one."

"Oh, I don't know. There are so many good ones. You pick one."

"Okay," I replied. "How about 'His Eye Is on the Sparrow'?"

My new friend was silent, her eyes averted. Then she fixed her eyes on mine again and said, "Yeah. Let's do that one."

She slowly nodded her head, put down her purse, straightened her jacket and faced the center of the shop. With my two-bar setup, she began to sing.

Why should I feel discouraged?
Why should the shadows come?

The audience of coffee drinkers was transfixed. Even the gurgling noises of the cappuccino machine ceased as the employees stopped what they were doing to listen. The song rose to its conclusion.

I sing because I'm happy;
I sing because I'm free.
For His eye is on the sparrow
And I know He watches me. . . .

When the last note was sung, the applause crescendoed to a deafening roar that would have rivaled a sold-out crowd at Carnegie Hall. Embarrassed, the woman tried to shout over the din, "Oh, y'all go back to your coffee! I didn't come in here to do a concert! I just came in here to get somethin' to drink, just like you!"

But the ovation continued. I embraced my new friend. "You, my dear, have made my whole year! That was beautiful!"

"Well, it's funny that you picked that particular hymn," she said.

"Why is that?"

"Well . . ." she hesitated again, "that was my daughter's favorite song."

"Really!" I exclaimed.

"Yes," she said, and then grabbed my hands. By this time, the applause had subsided and it was business as usual. "She was 16. She died of a brain tumor last week."

I said the first thing that found its way through my stunned silence.

"Are you going to be okay?"

She smiled through tear-filled eyes and squeezed my hands. "I'm gonna be okay. I've just got to keep trusting the Lord and singing his songs, and everything's gonna be just fine."

She picked up her bag . . . and then she was gone.

Was it just a coincidence that we happened to be singing in that particular coffee shop on that particular November night? Coincidence that this wonderful lady just happened to walk into that particular shop? Coincidence that of all the hymns to choose from,

I just happened to pick the very hymn that was the favorite of her daughter, who had died just the week before? I refuse to believe it.

God has been arranging encounters in human history since the beginning of time, and it's no stretch for me to imagine that he could reach into a coffee shop in midtown Manhattan and turn an ordinary gig into a revival. It was a great reminder that if we keep trusting him and singing his songs, everything's gonna be okay.

JOHN THOMAS OAKS
From *Christian Reader* magazine[4]

A Gentle Touch
For discussion or journaling

Wait on the LORD;
Be of good courage,
And He shall strengthen your heart;
Wait, I say, on the LORD!

PSALM 27:14

1. Describe your thoughts about Rick Warren's comparison between meditation and worry on pages 70–71.

2. One way to meditate on Scripture is an idea I read in a magazine article by Joanna Bloss.[5] Try reading six verses each day from Psalm 119 and writing down the blessings and benefits of knowing God's Word.

3. Do a quick review of this chapter. What is one idea that you can begin doing today that will help you become a woman who waits on and trusts in the Lord?

A Prayer from the Heart

Dear Lord,

How I long to lay aside my worries and put my trust more completely in You. Even as I wait for my prayers to be answered, help me to remember that You and You alone are the source of my comfort and hope. As I fall asleep each night, teach me to turn my worries into worship. I love You, Lord, with all my heart. I do love You.

CHAPTER 6

CUSHIONS
OF COMFORT

*God cushions our hurting hearts
with soft pillows of comfort and hope.*

JUDY GORDON

Nine years ago today, my mother stepped on heaven's shore. We were such good friends, and I miss her. I miss seeing her gray-blue eyes and the beauty of her deeply lined face. I miss holding her worn hands and hearing the sound of her low-pitched voice. But most of all, I miss my mother's comforting ways. She had been through so many sorrows of her own that it just came naturally for her to wrap her arms around someone who was hurting and to comfort them.

I often marveled at her—seemingly able to do just the right things without even thinking about it. While I was searching for something hopeful to say, I noticed that my mother's hugs and mingled tears spoke volumes more than any words. As intuitively as a new mother knows to rock her crying baby, my mother knew how to soothe someone's hurting heart. She understood a golden rule of conduct that is often overlooked: most people need a little bit of care and tenderness before they are ready for promises of hope.

When we're feeling low, in fact, hope often speaks most clearly in acts of love and comfort.

> *A cozy quilt.*
> *A listening ear.*
> *A gentle embrace.*
> *All are small*
> *givers of comfort.*
>
> AUTHOR UNKNOWN

My thesaurus associates *comfort* with words like *console, reassure, cheer, support, encourage, pamper, nourish,* and *refresh.* I love these words, don't you?

These are the kind of things that resonate within a woman's soul. They describe what we long to do for others when they are hurting and what we long to have someone do for us when our world falls apart. These are the cushions of comfort we all need when the blows of life are hard.

Once again I wish we were sitting alongside each other in some cozy little place, shoes kicked off, unhurried, talking about what comfort means. I would like to know your favorite ways of soothing and supporting others and what ways others have consoled or refreshed you. That's what this chapter is all about . . . snapshots of comfort, both giving and receiving. So kick off your shoes, curl up on the couch, grab a cup of tea, and let's exchange comfort stories.

The Gifts of a Friend

In *The Worn Out Woman*, I shared a story about Sally, a dear woman who discovered her husband was having an affair. Along with feeling betrayed and angry and scared, Sally felt like a failure. For days she carried her secret alone, not telling anyone because she was anxious about what people would think. But one morning at Bible study, her good friend Joan greeted Sally with a hug. "I've had you on my mind all week and was hoping to see you here today. How are you doing?" The dam broke, and Sally couldn't stop the tears. Joan pulled her into a private corner of the adjoining room and whispered, "Whatever it is, I promise you that no matter how long it takes I'll be here. I'll stand beside you whenever you need me."

A loving friend—what a source of comfort! Sharing your hurt with a trusted friend . . . or being that trusted friend to someone else . . . spontaneously opens the way to sprinkle glimmers of hope on dark and foreboding circumstances.

Joan stayed true to her promise. She set aside one morning

each week when she and Sally could take long walks together. During these times, Sally talked about her shattered dreams and her doubts that the marriage would survive. Joan avoided rushing in with advice. Mostly she listened. It was their habit to spend part of the time praying softly while they walked. Sometimes Joan would bring a Scripture promise that she had written on a piece of paper the night before and press it into her friend's hand when they said good-bye.

> *Encouragement is to a friendship what confetti is to a party. It's light, refreshing, and fun, and you always end up finding little pieces of it stuck on you later.*
>
> NICOLE JOHNSON

Joan remembered that Sally enjoyed the poetry of Robert Louis Stevenson and that among her favorites was "The Swing."

> How do you like to go up in a swing,
> up in the air so blue?
> Oh, I do think it the pleasantest thing
> ever a child can do![1]

Searching in used bookstores, Joan found just what she was looking for—a small illustrated volume of Stevenson's poems. She marked "The Swing" with a yellow silk ribbon and gave the book to Sally the next morning. Then, instead of going for their walk, they drove to the city park and spent the time swinging and laughing like two carefree little girls who didn't have a worry in the world.

In spite of his past unfaithfulness, Sally and her husband were gradually able to work through issues of trust and forgiveness, and their marriage survived. Through all the months of brokenness, Joan kept her promise and stood beside her friend for as long as she needed.

In thinking about their friendship, Joan demonstrated all the words that were listed in my thesaurus when I looked up the word *comfort*. I like to think that what Joan did was like giving gifts to her friend—gifts we all might consider giving when someone needs our support. To make it easy, I've summarized them into six items. At first glance they mostly look like gifts of comfort, but when they are unwrapped, there's always a bit of hope tucked inside:

- Give time
- Keep confidences
- Listen
- Pray
- Practice thoughtfulness
- Love faithfully

Family

Nancy Stafford, conference speaker, author, and actress on the television series *Matlock*, shares the following words about how she experienced comfort at home as a little girl:

When I was little, "In the Garden" was my mom's favorite hymn. Curled up in her lap, my head squooshed into her pillow-soft chest, I would rock with her in the brown nubby Ethan Allen rocker with the box pleat ruffle and the tiny creak in the spring.

Through earaches, scraped knees, and monsters under my bed, through schoolmate snubs, broken hearts, and piano recital fiascoes, this was my balm. We would rock together in the darkened living room . . . and all I heard was her. Singing to me. And singing to Jesus. Rocking in Mom's lap, wrapped in her arms and nestled into her chest, I learned what God's love and comfort feel like.[2]

What awesome opportunities we have in our families to imitate the nurture and grace of our heavenly Father; to extend open arms of support, reassurance, and hope; and to be keepers of a place called home where family members of any age can find safety and refreshment. These are the treasures of comfort a family can give.

In her book *In Every Pew Sits a Broken Heart*, Ruth Graham, daughter of Billy and Ruth Bell Graham, tells about a time when she received extraordinary comfort from her parents. Ruth (the daughter) had been through a divorce, married very soon afterward against everyone's advice, and then found her life in shambles once again. She writes, "I had caused pain for my children and loved ones. I feared I had embarrassed my parents. It seemed I had wrecked my world. The shame was almost unbearable."[3]

In a frantic moment, Ruth called her mother, who urged her to come home. Even though she dreaded what she might see in her parents' eyes, Ruth accepted the invitation because she desperately needed someone's comfort. Worried and exhausted from the sixteen-hour drive home, Ruth reached the top of her parents' steep driveway and spotted her father waiting for her.

Opening the car door, I barely had time to set foot on the asphalt before he was at my side. This dear father, who had every reason to rebuke, wrapped his strong arms around me, pulled me into a warm embrace, and greeted me with those simple words: "Welcome home."

My father's embrace at that moment was one of the most profound gestures of acceptance I have ever experienced. To be utterly broken and still accepted. To feel ugly and yet be loved. To feel like an outcast and still be welcomed. Unhesitatingly welcomed.[4]

Aren't the words "unhesitatingly welcomed" wonderful? They speak volumes about comfort. I think there must be a thirsty place deep inside every person that yearns for this kind of unconditional love. And I am convinced God created families to give and receive that kind of love.

The sad truth, of course, is that not every family lives up to the high calling of unconditional love. Perhaps your parents weren't good at nurturing or forgiving or even praying for you. Perhaps your family was or is a source of conflict rather than comfort. Or perhaps your family is simply absent. If this is true for you, you may need to look elsewhere for the family nurturing you need—to friends, to your church family, to the open arms of your heavenly Father.

And just as important, even if your family did not (or does not) treat you with kindness and support, you can still offer the comfort of love and acceptance to others. One of our dearest friends was abandoned by his parents, and for most of his young life raised in an uncaring and cruel foster home. And yet he and his wife and grown children are among the most compassionate and helpful people we have ever known.

Whether you are a mother, aunt, sister, or friend—and whether or not you have received comfort in your own family—you can still be like a mother hen, taking others under your wing and nestling them close with comfort and hope.

Chosen Comforters

"God has reasons behind my suffering, and learning some of them has made all the difference in the world. He has reasons for your suffering, too."[5]

If you have just heard devastating news about your health (or anything else for that matter) and someone with a broken toe spoke those words to you, they might sound thoughtless or cold-hearted. But once you knew they were written by Joni Eareckson Tada, who has been paralyzed from the neck down since she was seventeen years old, then the words might fall on your shoulders like a warm comforter on a winter day.

Words of hope and comfort seem softer if they are spoken by someone who has gone through times of difficulty. It makes a difference that their faith has been tested by fire—and they can still manage to speak words of loving encouragement.

Joyce, a friend in our Sunday Bible class at church, had a daughter who was killed in a car accident when she was twenty-four. For the past five years, Joyce has led a support group for mothers who have lost a child to death. The women who attend share memories, study Scripture, cry, and even find ways to laugh as they console one another. Each year the mothers host a candlelight service called "Lights of Love" to celebrate the lives and memories of their precious children.

Why do the mothers come? Why do they believe Joyce when she shares that one day the grief will lessen? Because she has been there.

Sheila Walsh cohosted *The 700 Club* with Dr. Pat Robertson for five years. Then one day she was admitted as a patient in the psychiatric wing of a hospital in Washington, D.C., diagnosed with severe clinical depression. Today she is a best-selling author and one of the Women of Faith conference speakers.

Why do we listen when Sheila talks about Christ's promise of healing? Why are we so encouraged when she shares how God brings beauty from ashes? Because she has been there.

My friend Karen is a ten-year survivor of breast cancer. Each year she organizes a group of women to walk in the Race for the Cure. She also completed training through a hospital program to be a first-contact resource person when other women are diagnosed with breast cancer, and she has started a support group for women who have cancer in the small community where she lives.

Why do women flock to Karen for comfort? Because she has been there.

I like to think of such people like Joyce and Sheila and Karen as God's chosen comforters. They are people uniquely qualified to minister God's comfort because they understand what difficulty is all about—and they also know firsthand the comfort that God provides.

That certainly explains why my own mother was such an effective comforter. Alcoholism, prison, mental illness,

> *Blessed be the God and Father of our Lord Jesus Christ, the Father of mercies and God of all comfort, who comforts us in all our tribulation, that we may be able to comfort those who are in any trouble, with the comfort with which we ourselves are comforted by God.*
>
> 2 CORINTHIANS 1:3–4

prodigals, out-of-wedlock pregnancy, poverty, divorce, long ill-nesses, and accidental death were some of the troubles that touched her precious little family. Through them all, her faith never wavered. In fact, it was through the most unbearable sorrows that my mother learned to trust Jesus the most.

She often said, "This too shall pass." And most of it did. In wondrous ways she saw the Good Shepherd rescue some of her lost lambs from dangerous and scraggly cliffs. For others, she waited and prayed all the more. A few weeks before she died, I told her that one of the things I would miss most was her prayers.

She took both of my hands in hers and just held them for the longest time, her eyes closed. When she opened them, she said, "If there is prayer in heaven, then always remember that I will never stop praying for my family."

Rick Warren could have been writing about my mother when he penned these words:

> *God never wastes a hurt!* In fact, your greatest ministry will most likely come out of your greatest hurt. Who could better minister to the parents of a Down syndrome child than another couple who have a child afflicted in the same way? Who could better help an alcoholic recover than someone who fought that demon and found freedom? Who could better comfort a wife whose husband has left her for an affair than a woman who went through that agony herself?[6]

It seems that part of the reason God allows us to go through painful experiences is to prepare us to minister to others. Rick Warren goes on to suggest that perhaps one of the best ways to discover how and where God wants you to serve is to ask yourself what problems, hurts, thorns, and trials you have learned from. What valley of sorrow have you walked through? Is there a way you can use that experience to help someone else? Remember that God has a very special place for you in His ever-widening circle of chosen comforters—a place that only you can fill.

God of All Comfort

You don't need to have experienced the exact same difficulty, of course, to comfort someone who is hurting. Imagination and empathy can help you put yourself in another's place, and you can trust the Holy Spirit to give you words and ideas when your own level of understanding is limited. Remember, comfort can be as simple as a hug or a Scripture verse written out and pressed into someone's hands.

And remember as well, that you are never expected to be *just* a comforter, just a giver, just a nurturer. God desires you to receive comfort too. You may find that comfort in the listening ears of treasured friends, in the embrace of a loving family, in the understanding faces of those who have walked through similar storms. You may find it in the pages of an uplifting book, the beauty of a sunrise, the soft nuzzle of a kitten. You will certainly find it in the pages of Scripture and the ever-present nearness of the Holy Spirit.

> If my life is broken when given to Jesus, it is because pieces will feed a multitude, while a loaf will satisfy only a little lad.
>
> RUTH STULL

However you experience it, the Lord is your ultimate source of comfort and hope.

Hebrews 4:15–16 tells us that Jesus Christ is our great High Priest who sympathizes with us and invites us to come boldly to Him in time of need. He is the One who has walked our valleys of sorrow and faced our fiercest storms. He knows what you are going through, and He longs for you to come to Him.

When you need someone to encourage, console, and support you,
    He invites you to come to Him.
When you need someone to wrap strong arms of protection around you,
    He invites you to come to Him.
When you need someone to put a promise of hope in your heart,
    He invites you to come to Him.
When you need someone to love you faithfully and unconditionally,
    He invites you to come to Him.
When you need someone to unhesitatingly welcome you home,
    He invites you to come to Him.
And when you come to Him, you will find a comfort that is greater,
    richer, wider, deeper, higher than any other.

The Comfort Room

I always love it when the path of author Mayo Mathers happens to cross mine. She is one of those rare women who seems like a close friend even if you have only met her a few times—most likely because she always seems so warm and welcoming. Snuggle in your favorite chair, breathe a deep sigh of contentment, and enjoy Mayo's heart of hospitality as you read her story.

"Is your Comfort Room available next weekend?" The voice of my friend on the telephone sounded weary and faint. "I could sure use a respite."

I smiled, assuring her it was. Hanging up the phone, I walked down the hall to the room she'd inquired about. The Comfort Room developed quite by accident, but there is no doubt in my mind that the people who stay here are no accident at all. God brings them to us when they're most in need of comfort.

I looked around the room, running my hand lightly across the soothing pattern of the wallpaper. Walking over to the antique bed, I stretched out across the quilt with its blue and white wedding ring pattern and luxuriated in the familiar sense of comfort that settled over me like a feathery eiderdown.

My earliest memory of the bed goes back to when I was three years old. My parents had just brought my new baby sister to Grandma's house where I'd been staying. As Mom laid her on the bed, I stood on my tiptoes, eagerly peeking over the high mattress to catch a glimpse of her.

For as long as I can remember, the bed and its accompanying dresser and dressing table occupied what had once been the parlor of my grandparents' large Missouri farmhouse. During those long-ago summers, when all the grandchildren visited, "taking turns" was the order of the day. We took turns on the porch swing, took turns on the bicycle, and even took turns at the chores. But there was no taking turns when it came to sleeping in Grandma's bed. Even on hot, smothery, summer nights she let us all pile in around her at once. Our sweaty little bodies stuck happily together as we listened to Grandma's beloved stories of the "olden days" until one by one, we fell asleep.

Those well-spun tales gave me a strong sense of family identity, pride, and comfort. And I needed plenty of comfort when clouds started building in the summery blue skies that stretched over the corn fields surrounding the farm. How I dreaded the wild, crashing, earsplitting midwestern thunderstorms that resulted from those massive clouds!

Standing at the window, I'd watch the lightning flashes intensify across the sky and count the seconds until I heard the low growl of thunder. Grandma told me that was how to tell how many miles away the storm was.

I hated nighttime storms the most—when I'd have to go upstairs to my bedroom, up even closer to the storm. Sleep was impossible. As the jagged slashes grew more brilliant, the time between the stab of lightning and the crash of thunder grew less and less.

Then suddenly, FLASH! KA-A-A-BOOM! The light and sound came as one! The storm was here! Right on top of me! At that point, I'd leap from the bed, and with my sister close behind, we'd slam into our brother in the hallway. The three of us tore down the stairs as one.

Hearing our pounding feet, Grandma would already be scooted over in bed with the covers thrown back for us. We plowed beneath them, scrunching up as close to her as we could. While the thunder shook and rattled the house, she'd jump dramatically and exclaim, "Whew! That one made my whiskers grow!" And from under the pillows where we'd buried our heads, we couldn't help but giggle. In Grandma's bed we were always comforted.

There I found comfort not only from thunderstorms but from lifestorms as well. Hurt feelings, broken hearts, insecurities—all were mended there. When I was lucky enough to have Grandma to myself in her bed—which wasn't often—I'd tell her all my deepest secrets, knowing she took them very seriously.

When my father, her son, died of cancer, I was eight years old. On that last night of his life, instead of spending those moments with him in the hospital, Grandma gathered me into her bed. Curling her body around mine, she infused me with comfort I didn't yet know I needed.

In college, when a broken engagement had crushed my heart and hopes, she comforted me by saying, "The pathway to love never runs smooth, honey, but you'll find your way when it's right." Four years later, her prediction came true.

Shortly after my wedding, Grandma died, bringing an end to the unlimited source of love and comfort that I knew could never be replaced, the kind that only comes from a grandmother.

The years melted away with startling speed. Caught up in the happy frenzy of raising our two sons, I rarely thought of the bedroom set stuck away in the attic. There was too much present to think of the past. Before I knew it, our firstborn was packing his belongings to move on to a new phase of life.

The day Tyler left, I went into his empty room and sat down in the middle of the floor while memory after memory scurried up to tap me on the shoulder. His leave-taking had been more wrenching than I had anticipated. Inside the echoes of the room I tried to come to grips with the door that had just closed on my life.

Quite abruptly, a thought came to mind. I raised my head and looked around my son's room with new eyes. I finally had room for Grandma's bedroom set!

For the next two weeks I worked on the room, lovingly choosing paint, wallpaper, and pictures. Frequent tears splashed into the paint tray as I pondered all the different seasons one passes through in a lifetime. When the painting and papering were done, my husband lugged the bedroom set down from the attic and helped me arrange it in the room. I stopped to consider the completed result and was drawn to the bed where I let my fingers trace around the grooves in the curved footboard of the wonderful old treasure. As I sat quietly, a familiar feeling begged to embrace me—the same feeling I'd had as a child with Grandma beside me in the bed. It was as if she were in the room with me right then comforting me in this new stage of life I was entering.

Right then I christened it the "Comfort Room." From where I sat I prayed, "Lord, I hope everyone who stays in this room feels the comfort I'm feeling now. Bring people to us who need the comfort."

Our first guest in the Comfort Room was a friend who'd just lost her brother and two close friends to death. Next was a couple who were at a transition point in their life, not sure which direction to go. Then a young cousin arrived in need of a temporary home and an out-of-town-uncle whose wife was flown to our medical center following a severe heart attack. From the day it was completed, God has seen to it that the Comfort Room is well used.

There is one guest, however, whose arrival I most anticipate. I'm waiting for the day when my son will return and bring with him a grandchild. Then I will be the grandma snuggling up with my grandchild in that old bed. I'll be the one spinning stories of the "olden days." And I'll offer to them what my grandma gave to me—unending comfort, unlimited love.

MAYO MATHERS
From *Today's Christian Woman* magazine[7]

A Gentle Touch
For discussion or journaling

You've kept track of my every toss and turn
through the sleepless nights,
Each tear entered in your ledger,
each ache written in your book.

PSALM 56:8
THE MESSAGE

1. Describe a time when someone did something special to comfort you or when you did something special to comfort someone else.

2. What problems, hurts, thorns, and trials have you learned from that might have prepared you to minister to others?

3. Think of someone who is hurting and to whom you can reach out this week. What might be your first step in doing this?

A Prayer from the Heart

Dear Lord,

You keep track of my tears—not one of them is overlooked or forgotten. Gently and sweetly You come and comfort me with precious words and tender reminders of Your compassion and love. As You have always comforted me, help me to reach out and comfort others who are hurting. Thank You, sweet Lord. Thank You.

Chapter 7

WHEN
PARENTS CRY

*It is because we continue to love
that we must sometimes continue to cry.*

JOY P. GAGE

The telephone rang just as the soft light of early morning began to peek through our bedroom window. And although I didn't feel the rushing panic that comes with midnight phone calls, a sense of melancholy settled around my heart even before I picked up the receiver. I sensed something was wrong. And I was right.

"Alice . . . Wendy's disappeared."

At first, Diane's voice was so flat, she sounded like she was reading from a cue card. However, the moment I said, "I'll be right over," her voice dissolved into tears.

"I've called all her friends," she whimpered. "This time she's really gone."

I had met Diane earlier that year at a group Bible study. One day she had asked me to lunch. And then, over sandwiches and iced tea, she had poured out her heart to me about her wayward daughter. A sophomore in high school, Wendy was failing in four of her classes, was cutting school at least once a week, and had started hanging out with some pretty scary kids. This was a girl who had been raised in a good Christian home and until recently had been involved with the youth group at church. Her parents and grandparents had started praying for her before she was born and had never stopped. And yet Wendy seemed to be slipping further and further away.

Diane had heard that I knew what it meant to have a child who wasn't walking with the Lord. And since I was about twenty years older than she was, she wanted my advice. Even more, she wanted my prayers. To this day, I don't remember what I said to encourage Diane, but I did promise to pray faithfully.

By the morning Diane called me, I had been praying three months, but the situation had grown steadily worse. Now Wendy had disappeared. Wendy had frequently sneaked home after curfew and had even "run away" before on two occasions, but it had been pretty easy to track her down with a few phone calls. This time, no one knew where she was.

Needless to say, Diane was frantic. All of us who knew her were deeply worried.

Was there still hope that everything would turn out okay?

A Parent's Dreams

A mother's yearnings for her children begin the moment she discovers she is pregnant. By the time she cradles her newborn son to her breast, she has already dreamed a hundred dreams about the fine young man he will become. Or when a mother rocks her little girl to sleep, she holds back tears as she imagines the goodness of her daughter's womanhood.

A few children do seem to glide into adulthood without apparent struggles. Others go through a few rough years before they start making good choices. But there are also children who seem to lose their way and to stay lost for a long time. They are "prodigals" like the son whose story is told in the Gospel of Luke, and they can cause a parent untold hours of grief and pain.

In his book *Parenting Isn't for Cowards,* Dr. James Dobson tells about a time he attended a wedding ceremony held in a beautiful garden setting. At the moment when the groom kissed his bride, 150 colorful, helium-filled balloons were released into the blue California sky. Dr. Dobson writes:

Within a few seconds, the balloons were scattered across the heavens—some rising hundreds of feet overhead and others cruising toward the horizon. The distribution was curious. They all began from a common launching pad, were filled with approximately the same amount of helium, and ascended into the same conditions of the sun and wind. Nevertheless, within a matter of several minutes they were separated by a mile or more. A few balloons struggled to clear the upper branches of trees, while the show-offs became mere pinpoints of color on their journey to the sky. How interesting, I thought—and how symbolic of children.[1]

Dr. Dobson continues with hopeful encouragement that even when kids go through some hard rebellious years, by the time they are in their mid-twenties, most have returned to the values of their parents. But that doesn't always happen, as you may well know. Our children have minds and wills of their own, and some will make choices that bring ongoing heartache.

Sometimes the child who has the most trouble getting off the ground eventually reaches the greatest height!

DR. JAMES DOBSON

Still Waiting

Maybe you are among the many parents who are still waiting for a child to come out of his or her rebellion—to finish their years of wild or promiscuous living.

You might be a parent whose child has left and taken a

part of your heart with him or her. You may not have had contact with your son or daughter for a long time, and on many nights you fall asleep on a pillow wet with tears. My own heart groans just thinking about the terrible pain you must feel.

Or perhaps you are a parent who has a different kind of heartache. You have contact with your kids, even share good times, but you are missing the joy of sharing kindred hearts—shared Christian fellowship. Your kids have different moral values, have grown spiritually cold. You may wonder if they really know Jesus Christ as Savior.

There is probably no deeper anguish than not knowing if a beloved son or daughter will be with you in heaven. Even if God has blessed you with many other good things, the longing for your children to know Christ as Lord is seldom, if ever, out of your thoughts. You may have waited and prayed for years and don't yet see the answer.

Prodigals are as new as tomorrow's headlines, as old as the Garden of Eden. For some reason they are usually thought of as teenage boys. But prodigals are not limited in gender, race, age, or color. They do have one thing in common: They have left home . . . and they are missed.

RUTH BELL GRAHAM

If this is where you are in life, please know that God shares your yearnings. He is waiting too. He loves your prodigal even more than you do!

If you are waiting for a child to come back from what the Bible calls "the far country," I would like to recommend to you a very tender book called *Prodigals: And Those Who Love Them*. Ruth Bell Graham, the wife of evangelist Dr. Billy Graham, wrote the book out of personal experience. As her daughter Gigi writes in the introduction, "Mother does know about prodigals, and this book reflects her search for God's comfort during those times in her life when her prodigals were running away from her love and care and only God could look out for them."[2]

Last year two mothers and I got together every few weeks to pray for our children and used Mrs. Graham's sensitive book for encouragement. I have so many pages marked in mine that it was really, really hard to choose only one excerpt to share with you. I finally decided to quote one of Mrs. Graham's poems:

> Listen, Lord,
> a mother's praying
> low and quiet:
> listen, please.
> Listen what her tears
> are saying,
> see her heart upon its knees;
> lift the load from her bowed shoulders
> till she sees and understands,
> You, who hold the worlds together,
> hold her problems
> in Your hands.[3]

Let me insert a word of hope here for all the parents who are still waiting for their prodigals. One of Ruth Bell Graham's beloved prodigals was her son Franklin, who spent quite a few years in rebellion against his upbringing. But Franklin's life was turned around, and he now heads up Samaritan's Purse, a Christian relief organization providing spiritual and physical aid to hurting people around the world. He also has assumed much of the preaching and leadership responsibilities at the Billy Graham Evangelistic Association.

The point is, you never know how the Lord will use your children's lives once He gets hold of their hearts. And that's a reality to hold tightly during those painful times of waiting and worry.

The Original Prodigal

If you are a parent who is still praying for your son or daughter to "come home," perhaps you are like me and get comfort from reading the parable that Jesus taught about the original prodigal son. No matter how often I read it, the happy ending always moves me. I especially like this modern paraphrase of Luke 15:11–24 from *The Message*:

> There was once a man who had two sons. The younger said to his father, "Father, I want right now what's coming to me."
>
> So the father divided the property between them. It wasn't long before the younger son packed his bags and left for a distant country. There, undisciplined and dissipated, he wasted everything he had. After he had gone through all his money, there was a bad famine all through that country and he began to hurt. He signed on with a citizen there who assigned him to his fields to slop the pigs. He was so hungry he would have eaten the corncobs in the pig slop, but no one would give him any.
>
> That brought him to his senses. He said, "All those farmhands working for my father sit down to three meals a

day, and here I am starving to death. I'm going back to my father. I'll say to him, Father, I've sinned against God, I've sinned before you; I don't deserve to be called your son. Take me on as a hired hand." He got right up and went home to his father.

When he was still a long way off, his father saw him. His heart pounding, he ran out, embraced him, and kissed him. The son started his speech: "Father, I've sinned against God, I've sinned before you; I don't deserve to be called your son ever again."

But the father wasn't listening. He was calling to the servants, "Quick. Bring a clean set of clothes and dress him. Put the family ring on his finger and sandals on his feet. Then get a grain-fed heifer and roast it. We're going to feast! We're going to have a wonderful time! My son is here—given up for dead and now alive! Given up for lost and now found!"

Isn't it a wonderful story? Every time I read through it, there seems to be something new. Like right now, when I typed it, I thought about the father and whether or not he regretted giving the son what he asked for. Maybe it had been a mistake, although surely, at the time, the father thought he was doing what was best for his son. He didn't know his son would take the money and live a dissipated life.

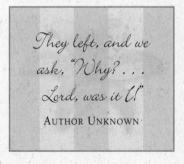

They left, and we ask, "Why? . . . Lord, was it I?"

AUTHOR UNKNOWN

I wonder how many times the father said to himself, *If only I had done things differently.* I know that thought often tiptoes—and sometimes stomps—across my heart.

Of course, when reading the parable, I'm always struck by the awesome example of the father's forgiveness . . . forgiveness that is given even before being asked. Not hesitating, not making forgiveness conditional, but restoring the wayward son to full status as his child and then celebrating with all the stops pulled out. Just think—that's what God does for us—and for our own beloved prodigals as well. When I read about that full-hearted forgiveness, I'm reminded how important it is to keep my own heart open, to strip myself of the natural anger or resentment that might grow during my times of waiting.

But you know what gives me the most hope from this parable today? It's the phrase "When he was still a long way off, his father saw him." You see, that tells me the father was *expecting* his son to come back home. Although it had been a long time, he hadn't given up. I think that's the kind of expectation we should have.

Can you just imagine how it was? Perhaps the first thing the father did each morning was to step outside and scan the horizon. Again near midday, he stopped whatever he was doing, putting his hand up to shade his eyes and searching the hillsides. Maybe, just before sunset, he took one more longing look before placing an oil lamp that would shine through the night in case his son came home while it was dark.

And then one afternoon, the father saw a figure approaching. Ragged clothes, disheveled hair, bony thin—but there was something familiar about his walk.

Could it be? Could this be his son coming home? With his heart pounding, the father ran to him. His son! His son who was lost! His son is now found!

If you are a parent whose son or daughter is still in the far country, maybe today will be the homecoming day.

Or maybe not today, but someday.

That's the bright ribbon of hope I find in this parable.

No matter how long it takes, keep praying, keep believing, keep expecting. I'm praying with you that one day soon we will see our prodigals come home.

As a hopeful postscript to this chapter, let me give you an update on Wendy, the girl at the beginning of this chapter.

Her parents found her after two agonizing days. But even though her entire family started going for counseling, Wendy continued to make some really poor choices, including dropping out of high school. She was like one of the balloons that Dr. Dobson described—struggling and tangled in the treetops. But eventually she did break free and began to soar. Wendy completed her GED and is currently attending community college.

Most important, Wendy has fallen in love with Jesus as Lord and Savior. Her mother says this verse from 2 Corinthians 5:17 best describes Wendy's life today: "Those who become Christians become new persons. They are not the same anymore, for the old life is gone. A new life has begun!"[4]

The Lovesick Father

Philip Yancey is an award-winning author. Many of his books have been on the best-seller list, and two received the Book of the Year award presented by the Evangelical Christian Publishing Association. I just know your heart will be touched by his story, which is actually a modern setting of the prodigal son story. It's one that I especially treasure.

A young girl grows up on a cherry orchard just above Traverse City, Michigan. Her parents, a bit old-fashioned, tend to overreact to her nose ring, the music she listens to, and the length of her skirts. They ground her a few times, and she seethes inside. "I hate you!" she screams at her father when he knocks on the door of her room after an argument, and that night she acts on a plan she has mentally rehearsed scores of times. She runs away.

She has visited Detroit only once before, on a bus trip with her church youth group to watch the Tigers play. Because newspapers in Traverse City report in lurid detail the gangs, the drugs, and the violence in downtown Detroit, she concludes that this is probably the last place her parents will look for her. California, maybe, or Florida, but not Detroit.

Her second day there she meets a man who drives the biggest car she's ever seen. He offers her a ride, buys her lunch, arranges a place for her to stay. He gives her some pills that make her feel better than she's ever felt before. She was right all along, she decides: her parents were keeping her from all the fun.

The good life continues for a month, two months, a year. The man with the big car—she calls him "Boss"—teaches her a few things that men like. Since she's underage, men pay a premium for her. She lives in a penthouse, and orders room service whenever she wants. Occasionally she thinks about the folks back home, but their lives now seem so boring and provincial that she can hardly believe she grew up there.

She has a brief scare when she sees her picture printed on the back of a milk carton with the headline "Have you seen this child?" But by now she has blond hair, and with all the makeup and body-piercing jewelry she wears, nobody would mistake her for a child. Besides, most of her friends are runaways, and nobody squeals in Detroit.

After a year the first sallow signs of illness appear, and it amazes her how fast the boss turns mean. "These days, we can't mess around," he growls, and before she knows it she's out on the street without a penny to her name. She still turns a couple of tricks a night, but they don't pay much, and all the money goes to support her habit. When winter blows in she finds herself sleeping on metal grates outside the big department stores. "Sleeping" is the wrong word—a teenage girl at night in downtown Detroit can never relax her guard. Dark bands circle her eyes. Her cough worsens.

One night as she lies awake listening for footsteps, all of a sudden everything about her life looks different. She no longer feels like a woman of the world. She feels like a little girl, lost in a cold and frightening city. She begins to whimper. Her pockets are empty and she's hungry. She needs a fix. She pulls her legs tight underneath her and shivers under the newspapers she's piled atop her coat. Something jolts a synapse of memory and a single image fills her mind: of May in Traverse City, when a million cherry trees bloom at once, with her golden retriever dashing through the rows and rows of blossomy trees in chase of a tennis ball.

God, why did I leave, she says to herself, and pain stabs at her heart. My dog back home eats better than I do now. She's sobbing, and she knows in a flash that more than anything else in the world she wants to go home.

Three straight phone calls, three straight connections with the answering machine. She hangs up without leaving a message the first two times, but the third time she says, "Dad, Mom, it's me. I was wondering about maybe coming home. I'm catching a bus up your way, and it'll get there about midnight tomorrow. If you're not there, well, I guess I'll just stay on the bus until it hits Canada."

It takes about seven hours for a bus to make all the stops between Detroit and Traverse City, and during that time she realizes the flaws in her plan. What if her parents are out of town and miss the message? Shouldn't she have waited another day or so until she could talk to them? And even if they are home, they probably wrote her off as dead long ago. She should have given them some time to overcome the shock.

Her thoughts bounce back and forth between those worries and the speech she is preparing for her father. "Dad, I'm sorry. I know I was wrong. It's not your fault; it's all mine. Dad, can you forgive me?" She says the words over and over, her throat tightening even as she rehearses them. She hasn't apologized to anyone in years.

The bus has been driving with lights on since Bay City. Tiny snowflakes hit the pavement rubbed worn by thousands of tires, and the asphalt steams. She's forgotten how dark it gets at night out here. A deer darts across the road and the bus swerves. Every so often, a billboard. A sign posting the mileage to Traverse City. Oh, God.

When the bus finally rolls into the station, its air brakes hissing in protest, the driver announces in a crackly voice over the microphone, "Fifteen minutes, folks. That's all we have here." Fifteen minutes to decide her life. She checks herself in a compact mirror, smoothes her hair, and licks the lipstick off her teeth. She looks at the tobacco stains on her fingertips, and wonders if her parents will notice. If they're here.

She walks into the terminal not knowing what to expect. Not one of the thousand scenes that have played out in her mind prepare her for what she sees. There, in the concrete-walls-and-plastic-chairs bus terminal in Traverse City, Michigan, stands a group of forty brothers and sisters and great-aunts and uncles and cousins and a grandmother and great-grandmother to boot. They're all wearing goofy party hats and blowing noise-makers, and taped across the entire wall of the terminal is a computer-generated banner that reads "Welcome home!"

Out of the crowd of well-wishers breaks her dad. She stares out through the tears quivering in her eyes like hot mercury and begins the memorized speech, "Dad, I'm sorry. I know . . ."

He interrupts her. "Hush, child. We've got no time for that. No time for apologies. You'll be late for the party. A banquet's waiting for you at home."

PHILIP YANCEY

From *What's So Amazing About Grace?*[5]

A Gentle Touch
For discussion or journaling

"For I know the plans I have for you," says the LORD. "They are plans for good and not for disaster, to give you a future and a hope."

JEREMIAH 29:11
NEW LIVING TRANSLATION

1. Read Mrs. Graham's poem again (page 105) and then write out your own prayer or poem for a child you love who is still in the far country. Or, if you prefer, write a prayer or poem about another type of concern.

2. What can you do to encourage someone else who has a rebellious child?

3. Is your heart forgiving and welcoming? How have you communicated this to your prodigal?

A Prayer from the Heart

Dear Lord,

I believe with all my heart that Your plans for my children and grandchildren are for good and not disaster. You want to give them a future and a hope. Please place hedges of protection around them—hedges that are high and thick so that they will not easily cross over to evil and so evil cannot easily cross over to them. I am thankful that even when they are out of my care, they are never out of Yours. Draw them to Yourself, Lord . . . soon.

Please, soon.

Chapter 8

HEARTBREAK HILL

When I run, I feel [God's] pleasure.

ERIC LIDDELL,
MISSIONARY AND OLYMPIC RUNNER

This past spring I observed an event that for more than one hundred years has taken place on the third Monday of every April. Twenty thousand athletes from all over the world had gathered in Boston, Massachusetts. The starter's gun fired, runners exploded from their positions, and the Boston Marathon was on.

The race is 26.2 miles from start to finish. And twenty-one miles into the race, the runners come to what is known as Heartbreak Hill. It is considered the most difficult part of the marathon. Even before they start up the hill, many of the runners are already exhausted. Dripping with sweat. Muscles cramping. Gulping for air. By the time they are midway up the hill, their body cries out: *Give up! Quit! It isn't worth it!* But they don't quit. They keep on running. Up and up. Pressing on and on toward the finish line.

Very simply, this is a picture of what God wants us to do in our lives. We also are in a race—not a sprint where we give it our all for a short dash, but a race of distance, discipline, and determination. And no matter how high the hills or how long the agony, God wants His children to press on and on toward the finish line.

Sound exhausting? Sometimes it is. Sometimes life does that to us.

This chapter is for those of you who have little hope that your particular heartbreak will ever be mended—for those whose marriage isn't reconciled, whose physical problem isn't getting better, whose prodigal hasn't returned, whose womb remains barren, and whose prayer seems to be unanswered. I have started and stopped a dozen times because whatever I write seems profoundly inadequate. I don't have satisfactory answers to all the whys and the what-ifs. And I'm afraid my words might sound trite or uncaring for someone who is straining to reach the top of Heartbreak Hill.

Today when I was talking to Larry Gadbaugh, a pastor friend, I asked him about hope for hopeless situations. He said, "That's when hope becomes stretched-out faith." He explained that sometimes hope must stretch beyond a world where there aren't always happy endings to a place where the One who loves us the most wipes away our tears. A place where there's no such thing as heartbreak.

> *The anchor of hope is sunk in heaven, not on earth.*
> GREGORY FLOYD

The Overlooked Gift

Larry and I talked awhile longer, and I shared with him something that I had just read in a little book by John R. Claypool called *The Hopeful Heart*. Dr. Claypool, who has endured a number of traumas, including the loss of his ten-year-old daughter to leukemia, writes gently yet eloquently of those times in our lives when hope fades or seems lost altogether. He affirms that God gives grace to help in even these dark times—and that this may happen in any of three distinct ways.

The first way God may choose to help is through a miracle—an amazing and circumstance-altering turn of events with no human or physical explanation. God really does do that from time to time. And even though such miracles are rare, why shouldn't we hope for them? Most of us were raised on the miracles of the Bible, and it is only natural that we should want God to rescue us and the ones we love in such a spectacular way.

But the truth is, it doesn't usually happen like that. More often, it seems, God bestows His grace in a second way, collaborating with us and others to bring about a good result. This could happen through the discovery of a new medical treatment, the opening of a door for employment, the infusion of an innovative idea, the bestowing of unexpected resources. God's ways of partnering with humankind are far too numerous to list, but perhaps we need to be more aware that when something wrong turns out right, it is because God has shared His grace with us.

And there is a third way that God helps, one that is less obvious. "These are the times," as Dr. Claypool points out, "when God seems to be saying, 'There will be no solving of the problem, but I will give you the strength to endure the unchangeable.'"[1] Claypool refers to this particular form of divine help as the "often overlooked gift." I suspect it is also the least wanted one—that is, until we discover its treasure.

Of course, as soon as I shared these thoughts about endurance with my pastor friend, we started talking about

> *I hope I can be an example that God wants us to trust in the good times and the bad. For if we don't trust when times are tough, we don't trust at all.*
>
> A WOMAN NAMED GLYN, SHORTLY BEFORE DYING OF LOU GEHRIG'S DISEASE

Hebrews 11 and 12. Hebrews 11 is that great chapter in the Bible about men and women who down through the ages endured terrible hardships and yet remained faithful—people like Noah, Abraham, Sarah, Moses, David, and other un-named heroes "of whom the world was not worthy." Then chapter 12 begins with a reminder that these faithful souls are like spectators in a vast arena cheering us on as we run the race of our lives:

> Therefore, since we have so great a cloud of witnesses sur-rounding us, let us also lay aside every encumbrance and the sin which so easily entangles us, and let us run with endurance the race that is set before us, fixing our eyes on Jesus, the author and perfecter of faith, who for the joy set before Him endured the cross, despising the shame, and has sat down at the right hand of the throne of God. For consider Him who has endured such hostility by sinners against Himself, so that you will not grow weary and lose heart.[2]

The very first time I taught a Bible study on this passage, I started researching distance running, which I knew next to nothing about. I interviewed runners, read articles, and even tried self-training to run a marathon. (That didn't last long!) Through my interviews, I discovered many valuable insights about why the writer of Hebrews compared the Christian life to a long race. Here are just a few things I gleaned from my interviews.

Thin-Clads and Seaweed

Distance runners sometimes refer to themselves as thin-clads because they wear such abbreviated, lightweight clothing. In order to run better, they try to get rid of everything that might weigh them down—even their shoes are featherweight.

Could this be what the writer of Hebrews means by "Lay aside every encumbrance"? Because we don't use it every day, *encumbrance* seems like an odd word, but it just means anything that hinders or impedes. The unnecessary. Whatever might distract from a goal or slows down our progress.

Each of us has our own encumbrances. For some it might be worry, regrets, fear. For others anger, unforgiveness, bitterness. Or busyness, perfectionism, envy. Whatever is hindering our faith, we aren't thin-clads until we lay it aside.

What else are we to put aside? "The sin which so easily entangles us."

The last time I walked along the beach, talking with a friend, watching the waves, not paying much attention where I was going, I tripped on a mound of wet seaweed. Yuck! Little creatures came flying out. The seaweed was smelly and slimy and stuck to my feet. That's kind of how it is when we get entangled with sin—especially when we aren't paying attention.

Can you imagine what it would feel like to be running a race and step in such a mess? If it were me, I'd fall flat on my face and forget where I was going in the first place.

How do we get rid of this entangling sin? As Christians, we all have a desire to resemble Christ as much as humanly possible. When I wonder if something I'm doing or saying or thinking falls in the sin category, I ask myself if it is something that resembles what Christ would do. And then this often-told little story helps me get untangled.

A sculptor once fashioned a magnificent lion out of solid stone. When asked how he had accomplished this wonderful masterpiece, he replied, "It was easy. I kept chipping away everything that didn't resemble a lion."

And so it is with us. To run a race of endurance we need to get rid of everything in our life that doesn't resemble Christ—sin, encumbrances, and all.

What Keeps Us Running?

One of the most valuable insights I learned from interviewing distance runners was that many experience what they call "hitting a runner's wall." At some point during a marathon, they feel like there is an invisible wall in front of them, and they want to give up. It just seems impossible to finish the race.

Because this same sort of thing happens to Christians when they feel hopeless, I wanted to find out what kept the runners in the race when they came to a wall and wanted to quit. That's why I went to the Boston Marathon—to interview runners after they came across the finish line.

Remember, these were people who had just run 26.2 miles. Many were trembling from the sheer shock of what their bodies had endured, and first-aid volunteers were wrapping thermal blankets around them to help. Other runners stumbled across the line and then fell on the ground, holding their sides and curling up their legs in a fetal position. Some were bent double, throwing up. And still others were absolutely exhilarated—arms lifted high in victory and tears, wonderful, joyful tears streaming down their cheeks.

I had just one question for all of them. What kept you running? And the answers I received fell into three distinct categories. When you read what they are, you might get a better sense of how the gift of endurance actually plays out in our lives—and how you can survive those times when you're up against a runner's wall in your own life-race.

Answer #1: "You see this picture pinned to my jersey? That's why I kept running."

Some of the pictures I saw that day were of a young wife who had died from cancer, a boy in a wheelchair, the twin towers that fell on September 11, 2001, and a marine standing proud with his hand touching his forehead in a salute.

Many of the runners raced because they were honoring someone they loved, and that was reason enough for them to keep running. When our times are the most hopeless, maybe our love for the Lord will be reason enough to keep us running too.

Answer #2: "I kept on running because people were cheering me on."

At a marathon the spectators don't just cheer at the start and finish line. You can see people cheering all along the course—especially at the hardest points of the race. At Heartbreak Hill in Boston, the crowd was sometimes three or four deep. Every time a runner came in sight, a cheer rose from the sidelines. If a runner was struggling, sometimes a spectator would step out and run alongside that person for a while, offering a cup of water and shouting words of encouragement.

It was thrilling!

Maybe this is why it's so important to be part of a local church, be involved in small groups, and have Christian friends. Sometimes we need someone to cheer us on so we will keep running.

Answer #3: "I kept running for the thrill of crossing the finish line."

I heard this answer more than any other. When they hit the runner's wall, they persevered for the absolute joy that comes with finishing.

I believe this is what the writer of Hebrews is trying to teach us when He speaks of "fixing our eyes on Jesus, the author and perfecter of faith, who for the joy set before Him endured the cross." Christ was looking beyond this life to a joy far greater than anything this world can offer. That's exactly what my pastor friend meant when he talked about a hope that stretches past our world with so many unhappy endings to a place where there will be no more tears or heartbreaks.

> *No matter how tough life gets, if you can see the shore (of heaven) and draw your strength from Christ, you'll make it.*
>
> RANDY ALCORN

Eyes on the Goal

When author and conference speaker Carole Mayhall received the first painful news of her sister's battle with cancer, she launched on a determined search for godly wisdom. As it turned out, her search for God's wisdom became more of a search to know Him—who He is and how He works in our lives. A story she tells in her book *Lord, Teach Me Wisdom* beautifully illustrates the need to keep our eyes on the finish line when tough times shatter our happiness:

The other night [my husband] Jack and I watched a television drama called "See How She Runs." The story concerned a 40-year-old divorced teacher from Boston who decided to become a jogger, and eventually entered the 26-mile Boston

Marathon. To finish the race became her goal, and in spite of being harassed, jeered at, and assaulted, she did not lose sight of it. The day of the race came and she faced her ultimate test. As she ran, huge blisters developed on her feet. She was also hit and injured by a bicycle. And several miles short of the finish line found her utterly exhausted. Yet she kept going. Then, within a few hundred yards of the finish line, late at night when most other runners had either finished or dropped out, she fell and lay flat on her face, too tired to raise her head. But her friends had put up a crude tape across the finish line and began to cheer her on. She lifted her head with great effort, saw the tape, and realized her goal was within sight. With a supreme effort she got up on her bruised and bleeding feet, and in a burst of energy dredged up from deep inside her courageous heart, she ran the last few yards.

She had kept her eyes on the goal and for the joy of finishing, she endured.[3]

The Gift of the Finish

In Boston, just a few yards from the finish line, I saw a runner start to crumple. It didn't seem like she was going to make it. But at that moment, another runner came alongside and held her up, almost carrying her across the finish line.

For me, this was a beautiful example of what Jesus does for us when we have exhausted all our strength. He comes alongside and holds us up with the gift of endurance so that we can keep running. And if our heartbreak hills are too high and the struggles too long, He does more than hold us up. He carries us.[4] He makes sure we can finish. And that, indeed, *is a gift to treasure.*

Race on, my friend. Race on and on and on . . . to joy!

A Man Named Winterhawk

Winterhawk Semler (his real name!) was the first runner I ever interviewed. Not only did he leave an indelible mark on my life, he truly helped me understand what it means to run the race of faith without losing heart—or hope.

Winterhawk didn't particularly look like a distance runner. Oh, he was clean-cut enough, but his huge, muscular arms and bearded face somehow reminded me more of a mountain man than a fleet-footed athlete. During the weekdays Winterhawk—or Hawk, as his friends called him—worked as the groundskeeper for the school district in the small community where we lived. But on the weekends and in the evenings, Winterhawk trained for ultramarathons. He ran one-hundred-mile races with a goal to finish in less than twenty-four hours.

Around our town, everyone knew that Winterhawk was a runner, and everyone knew he loved kids. When he wasn't running his own races, Hawk volunteered at cross-country and other track events and donated his time to help raise money for needy children. There's a bark-dust running trail around the middle school that he designed; years later, the school district named it Hawk's Trail in honor of his work with kids.

One morning when I was preparing to teach a Bible study class and needed some insights on Hebrews 12:1–3, I called the high-school track coach and asked whom I might interview for information. Unhesitatingly Coach Cook said, "You've got to talk to Hawk."

We met in a warehouse-sized garage surrounded by tractors and mowers. After offering me the only chair, Winterhawk moved some papers around and then settled comfortably on the corner of an old wooden desk. Although I had heard about this man's generosity and compassion, I was surprised to see such an obvious kindness reflected in his eyes.

Winterhawk wasn't a Christian, but he seemed thoroughly interested in the Hebrews 12 verses that use running a race as an analogy for endurance, and he enthusiastically answered all my questions. When I asked about "laying aside every encumbrance," he explained that distance runners run as light as they can. Even their shoes are constructed for lightness as well as endurance.

When we got to the verse about how sin can sidetrack Christians, Winterhawk easily made the connection to running. He said that runners had to be watchful all the time, or they could trip on something small like a little pebble, pull a muscle, and be out of the race. Then he added that the biggest risk is running in the dark. I volleyed with the idea that in the book of Psalms, the Bible is referred to as a light on our path and in the New Testament Jesus is called the Light of the World.

Back and forth we went for almost an hour. What great analogies he gave me. Finally, I had just one more question before ending the interview. Up until that moment, Winterhawk quickly answered everything. But when I asked, "What is it like to finish a race?" he paused before answering. Looking away—his thoughts seemed to take him outside the warehouse-sized garage to a place where runners' shoes rhythmically stroked the trail. When he turned back, his eyes still looked kind. But there was another dimension as well— something full of warmth and wonder.

"I've never been asked that question before," he said thoughtfully.

"Most people ask about winning—but you see, to a distance runner, finishing is the victory."

He said he couldn't find the right words to describe his feelings. It gave him goose bumps just to think about it. He couldn't explain because no one knew the cost—all he had to go through just to finish. Then Winterhawk looked me straight in the eye and said, "Alice, you will have to become a runner to understand."

Once again we talked about how his words paralleled running the Christian race. As with a distance runner, finishing is victory.

I told Winterhawk that I, too, could not find the words to describe what it meant to me to finish my race well. It gave me goose bumps just to think about it. I could not explain because no one knew what I would have to go through just to finish well—no one except Jesus Christ.

One day, I told him, my race will take me to the final finish line. Christ will be there, His arms open wide, calling, "This way, Alice. This way. Run toward Me." And He will embrace me and welcome me, "Well done, my good and faithful one. Well done."

What a finish line! What a victory! What a homecoming!

Then I looked Winterhawk straight in the eye and said, "Winterhawk, I guess you will have to become a Christian to understand."

I only saw Winterhawk three more times. A month or so after the interview, my husband and I met with him for the purpose of sharing how we had come to believe in Jesus Christ as our Savior. When we finished, Winterhawk wasn't ready to make a decision about what he believed, but he said he would give it a lot of thought. We gave him our phone number and said that if he had any questions, we would love to get together again. Before we left, we gave him a modern-paraphrase Bible that had a photograph of a distant runner on the same page as Hebrews 12. When Winterhawk thanked us, he commented that since the first time we met, he never ran without thinking about that passage.

The next time I saw Winterhawk was when he was doing a hundred-mile charity run to help children. It was a run of continuous laps around the high-school track for twenty-four hours. He was the only runner in the event, but from time to time his wife, Becky, or one of his friends would run some laps with him. I went to cheer him on. When I arrived, it was dark and he was exhausted but determined to finish.

My last meeting with Winterhawk was when we bumped into each other at the post office right before Christmas. As we waited in line, we visited like long-lost friends: What was happening in our lives? What were our plans for Christmas? How was his running? And before we said good-bye, I asked, "How are things with you spiritually? Have you thought any more about Jesus Christ?"

"Yes, and I'm pretty close to making a decision. Lately I keep meeting people who talk about their faith the same way you do. Is it really that simple—just believing in Christ?"

"Yes, my friend. It really is that simple."

A quick hug. Merry Christmas. I'll see you sometime soon.

We got the sad news a few months later: Winterhawk had been killed in an automobile accident. His wife was with him, and some say Winterhawk saw the truck coming toward them and swerved his vehicle so he, not Becky, would take the brunt of the crash. However it happened, in my heart I see Winterhawk running toward that final finish line. He's looking up, and Christ is there with arms open wide, calling, "This way, Winterhawk. This way. Run toward Me."

ALICE GRAY

A Gentle Touch
For discussion or journaling

> But those who wait on the LORD
> Shall renew their strength;
> They shall mount up with wings like eagles,
> They shall run and not be weary,
> They shall walk and not faint.

ISAIAH 40:31

1. Look at the list of suggested encumbrances in the second paragraph on page 123. What would you add to the list? Which is the one that weighs you down the most?

2. Thinking back to the example of the sculptor and the lion, what in your life doesn't resemble Christ? Are you willing to chip it away?

3. In this chapter, the strength of endurance is referred to as the often-overlooked gift, the least wanted gift, and the treasured gift. Choose one of these and write a few sentences describing why you think it is the best definition.

A Prayer from the Heart

Dear Lord,

When my heartbreak hills seem too high and the struggles seem too long, please wrap Your arms around me and hold me up. Give me the strength to endure without growing weary because, dear Lord, I want to please You. I want to feel Your pleasure when I run.

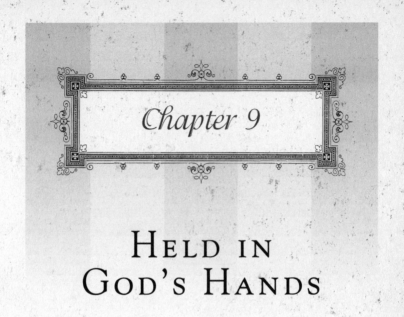

Chapter 9

HELD IN
GOD'S HANDS

And, Lord, please don't let me ever forget . . .
This is not the end of the story.

PAM BRADSHAW,
MANDY'S MOTHER

E very so often, thoughts of Mandy tiptoe across my heart. Whenever I think of her, I am both inspired and moved to tears.

I first "met" Mandy when I read a story about her by Eva Marie Everson.[1] Then I heard about her Web site and learned even more about her. I still visit the site from time to time to find out what is happening in Mandy's life, and each visit brings me a little infusion of hope.

At nineteen, Mandy loved the Lord, had an infectious sense of humor, sang in the worship team at her church, and wore a small band of white gold on her left ring finger. This attractive young woman wasn't married—the gold band was a promise ring engraved with the words *True Love Waits*. It represented her testimony to others and her promise to God to stay sexually pure until married.

On an August evening, Mandy and her friend were on their way to church when a man driving in the opposite direction suffered a seizure. His car veered out of control, crossed over several lanes of traffic, and hit Mandy's car broadside. The friend was rescued with only minor injuries, but Mandy's arm was severed and she suffered a severe head injury that plunged her into a coma.

Eva Marie Everson wrote, "Over the next twenty-two weeks Mandy miraculously survived pneumonia, staph infection, and major surgery to remove a piece of IV tubing that had snapped loose and lodged in her heart. All the while, as she lay helpless in the cupped hands of God, the faith of all who love her grew from mustard seeds to mountains!"

Today, more than five years later, Mandy still rests in God's cupped hands. Paralyzed from the neck down, she lives at home, lovingly cared for by family and friends. Medical paraphernalia dominates her otherwise cheerful room, and when she is lifted out of bed, a specially designed wheelchair supports her head. Although she cannot communicate with words, her smile lights up the room when she recognizes someone—and she chuckles whenever anything funny happens.

This morning, when I visited Mandy's Web site, I noticed that more than sixteen thousand visitors have found their way—some by "accident" and others by intention—to this oasis of hope. Messages for Mandy include phrases like these:

- "We found this Web site and cried and rejoiced and cried and prayed. Thank you."
- "The prayers still continue. May we never lose sight of the fact that we serve a good and faithful God."
- "Even when we forget, He carries us. When we blink, He does not."
- "We will pray for your peace and knowledge that in this time of trial, God is in control and has a plan and a reason for what is happening."
- "I am caring at home for my thirty-two-year-old son Jeffrey, who has profound physical and mental disabilities from birth. God bless you in your journey!"
- "Your life touched mine in so many ways."
- "In the greenest of valleys, the highest of hills; the Lord watches over us."
- "Please never stop believing and praying—that's where the true miracle is."
- "I pray for you every night and morning."

After reading just a portion of the hundreds of posted messages, I was choked with tears. When my husband came in to see how my writing was going, I tried to read some of the messages to him but was so touched I couldn't get the words out.

In spite of what we call tragic circumstances, Mandy's life continues to have profound influence, and the mustard seeds of faith are still growing as big as mountains.

Unraveling the Mystery

For me, the reasons why God allows prolonged illnesses and disabilities are mysteries. Sometimes incomprehensible tragedy descends on innocent babies still being knit together in their mother's womb or on young men and women with a world of dreams waiting to be conquered. At other times, aged ones who long for the freedom of heaven find instead that they are confined for years with broken bodies or withered minds. And as they linger, they ask daily, "Why? Why does God leave me here?"

Great theologians have debated these mysteries for centuries without coming up with satisfactory answers that cover every question. Even when we

> The Father has not lost track of your circumstances, even though they seem to be swirling out of control. He is there. Hold on to your faith in the midst of these unanswered questions. Someday His purposes will be known.
>
> DR. JAMES DOBSON

accept that some mysteries won't be solved until we see Jesus face to face, it can still be hard to hang on to hope when God and our circumstances don't seem to make sense. Those times when life seems sorrowfully unfair give us the greatest tests of our faith. We hope and pray for miracles, but most often the "big" miracles don't happen and we are left with a choice of how to respond.

In his book *When God Doesn't Make Sense*, Dr. James Dobson tells about a pastor whose fifteen-year-old daughter, Becki, was diagnosed with a malignant tumor. The doctors feared they would have to amputate one of her legs. But Pastor Jim Conway refused to believe that God would allow this to happen. Instead, he began praying for a miracle. Not only did he pray, but he also garnered the prayers of thousands of others around the world. His church held a twenty-four-hour vigil of fasting and prayer, and Pastor Conway was thoroughly convinced that Becki's leg would be saved. On the day the amputation was scheduled, he asked the doctor to be prepared to halt the surgery and instead verify that the cancer had been healed.

When the amputation was performed as scheduled, Pastor Conway felt spiritually abandoned and tumbled into a deep pit of despair. He wasn't just angry with God; his faith was shattered. But after months of working through resentment, frustration, and depression, Pastor Conway was able to write:

> Probably the most important thing I learned in this entire process is this: I became deeply aware that there were only two choices that I could make. One was to continue in my anger at God and follow the path of despair I was on. The other choice was to let God be God, and somehow say, "I don't know how all this fits together. I don't understand the

reasons for it. I'm not even going to ask for the explanation. I've chosen to accept the fact that You are God and I'm the servant, instead of the other way around." And there I left it.

It was in that choice that I came to cope with my situation. . . . I have come to recognize that God has a higher purpose and I just don't understand that purpose. I am prepared to wait until eternity to receive answers to my questions, if necessary. Like Job, I am now able to say, "Though he slay me, yet will I trust him" (Job 13:15 KJV). It's either despair, or it's the acceptance of His sovereignty. Those are the alternatives.

Let me say it again. It's either despair, or it's God. There's nothing in between. Our family has chosen to hold on to God.[2]

Somehow, even though their lives took a terrible turn, both Pastor Conway and Mandy's family have managed to unravel part of the mystery. They have come to realize that the true object of their faith isn't good health and smooth sailing. It isn't miracles or answered prayer. They set their hearts and minds on the One who is higher, greater, and more wonderful than any of these things. They chose trust instead of despair, and this choice has transformed them so profoundly that they no longer need or desire all the answers. Their faith is grounded in the Word of God, and that is enough. Theirs is the treasured faith defined in Hebrews 11:1: "the substance of things hoped for, the evidence of things not seen."

God's Chariots

When Christ walked the dusty roads of earth, He healed everyone who asked. His miracles and signs and wonders were a testimony for an unbelieving world and a sign of hope for those who followed Him. With a touch of His hand or a word from His lips, sight was restored, leprosy was cleansed, and broken bodies were made whole.

Christ still heals today too, but He does not heal everyone who asks—or at least not the *way* we expect. For some, He gives a different kind of healing miracle—a miracle of strength, perseverance, character, and hope.

Even though the outcome may be different from what is expected, the unbelieving world still sees a testimony. They see someone who is suffering and yet sings God's praises. They see someone who is brokenhearted and yet trusts the Lord completely. They see someone who experiences terrible losses and yet holds on to tremendous peace. When they observe, they do not forget. Many find their hearts forever changed.

Something changes in my own life as well when I consider the unwavering faith of people who endure extreme suffering. My thoughts are more contemplative, and my heart is bowed more reverently before the King of kings.

Not long ago I read of a Christian man who became a quadriplegic at the age of eighteen, when he was injured by a bullet. Over the years, many people have said to him, "I bet you are looking forward to heaven so that you can walk and run and jump." Although he never corrects them, in the privacy of his home he whispers to his wife that he is looking forward to heaven not because he will be able to walk and run and jump, but because then he will be able to kneel.[3]

Last Sunday in church, we were singing one of Isaac Watt's great hymns.

> Alas! And did my Savior bleed
> And did my Sovereign die?
> Would He devote that sacred Head
> For sinners such as I?[4]

And as I grasped the reality behind those powerful words, I found I could not remain seated. With tears rolling down my cheeks—and thinking of the example of that paralyzed young man, I quietly slipped to my knees.

Oh, dear ones like Mandy and Pastor Conway and the quadriplegic man who longs to kneel in heaven and so many, many more of you who suffer but do not lose faith—I hope you know how deeply you are touching our lives. You are helping us to grow our mustard seeds of faith and teaching us to hope even when the way is dark and stormy.

It might only be a small comfort, but we want you to know that you are like God's chariots, carrying us to a higher place of worship.

Significance

Joni Eareckson Tada, who has been a quadriplegic since 1967, is an international conference speaker and the founder and president of Joni and Friends, which has distributed more than twenty-five thousand wheelchairs to developing nations, where they are distributed to needy children and adults. (You can read more about this effort on Joni's Web site, www.joniandfriends.org.) Because of her role as a disability advocate, she received a presidential appointment and served on the National Council on Disability for three and a half years. She is the best-selling author of more than thirty books, including Secret Strength *and* Ordinary People, Extraordinary Faith.

Every morning Connie opens Diane's door to begin the long routine of exercising and bathing her severely paralyzed friend.

The sun's rays slant through the blinds, washing the room in a soft, golden glow. The folds of the covers haven't moved since Connie pulled them up around Diane the night before. Yet she can tell her friend has been awake for a while.

"Are you ready to get up yet?"

"No . . . not yet," comes the weak reply from under the covers. Connie sighs, smiles, and clicks shut the door.

The story is the same each dawn of every new day at Connie and Diane's apartment. The routine rarely changes. Sunrise stretches into midmorning by the time Diane is ready to sit up in her wheelchair. But those long hours in bed are significant.

In her quiet sanctuary, Diane turns her head slightly on the pillow toward the corkboard on the wall. Her eyes scan each thumbtacked card and list. Each photo. Every torn piece of paper carefully pinned in a row. The stillness is broken as Diane begins to murmur.

She is praying.

Some would look at Diane—stiff and motionless—and shake their heads. She has to be fed everything, pushed everywhere. The creeping limitations of multiple sclerosis encroach further each year. Her fingers are curled and rigid. Her voice is barely a whisper. People might look at her and say, "What a shame. Her life has no meaning. She can't really do anything."

But Diane is confident, convinced her life is significant. Her labor of prayer counts.

She moves mountains that block the paths of missionaries.

She helps open the eyes of the spiritually blind in southeast Asia.

She pushes back the kingdom of darkness that blackens the alleys and streets of the gangs in east L.A.

She aids homeless mothers . . . single parents . . . abused children . . . despondent teenagers . . . handicapped boys . . . and dying and forgotten old people in the nursing home down the street from where she lives.

Diane is on the front lines, advancing the gospel of Christ, holding up weak saints, inspiring doubting believers, energizing other prayer warriors, and delighting her Lord and Savior.

This meek and quiet woman sees her place in the world; it doesn't matter that others may not recognize her significance in the grand scheme of things. In fact, she's not unlike Emily in *Our Town* who signs her address as:

Grovers Corner
New Hampshire
United States of America

Western Hemisphere
Planet Earth
Solar System
The Universe
Mind of God

In the mind of God . . . that's about as significant as you can get, whether you sit at a typewriter, behind the wheel of a bus, at the desk in a classroom, in a chair by your kitchen table, or lay in bed and pray. Your life is hidden with Christ. You enrich His inheritance. You are His ambassador. In Him your life has depth and meaning and purpose, no matter what you do.

Someone has said, "The point of this life . . . is to become the person God can love perfectly, to satisfy His thirst to love. Being counts more than doing, the singer more than the song. We had better stop looking for escape hatches, for this is our hatchery."

It's my prayer that . . . you will discover the significance that has been yours all along as a child of the King. You may not be able to know the full meaning of every event, but you can know that every event is meaningful.

And you are significant.

JONI EARECKSON TADA
From *Glorious Intruder* [5]

A Gentle Touch
For discussion or journaling

I cried out to the LORD in my suffering, and he heard me.
    He set me free from all my fears. . . .
Taste and see that the LORD is good.
    Oh, the joys of those who trust in him!

PSALM 34:6, 8
NEW LIVING TRANSLATION

1. Have you ever been in a situation where you felt you had only two choices—to despair or to hold on to God? What did you choose, and what were the results?

2. Think of someone you know or have read about who struggled with a long-term illness or disability. How did this person's life affect you in a positive way?

3. What part of the ending story by Joni Eareckson Tada had the biggest impact on you . . . and why?

A Prayer from the Heart

Dear Lord,

Thank You for reminding me that even when incomprehensible tragedies happen, life still has depth and meaning and purpose. A person whose life is broken or marred is no less precious to You. Sometimes Your ways are beyond my comprehension, but You are never beyond my worship. You are worthy, O Lord. You are forever worthy of my praise.

Chapter 10

JOURNEY OF HOPE

Funny, I don't feel sad about going home.
I do pray for strength for the journey.

BARBARA BAUMGARDNER

Everyone who knows my dear friend Barbara Baumgardner wants to spend more time with her. Her deep faith in God, winsome personality, and caring heart make even strangers feel like they are welcome friends. For Barbara, life is an adventure. Although she had been a widow for almost twenty years, it didn't keep her from buying a new motor home when she turned sixty-seven and driving it all over the country. Barbara loved discovering back roads and out-of-the-way places. Soon she had become a featured columnist for *RV Companion* magazine, writing about the places she visited and the people she met.

Last summer, Barbara had surgery to remove a malignant tumor. Then, as soon as she was declared cancer free, she began planning her next trip. As a precaution, however, she insisted on one more CAT scan before climbing in her motor home and heading for the open road once again.

Toward the end of January, Barbara telephoned to tell me about her latest plans.

"Alice, I'm calling to tell you about the best adventure yet," she chirped.

Knowing Barbara's zest for fun, I could hardly wait to hear what she was planning this time. Nothing in her upbeat enthusiasm prepared me for the news she shared that morning.

The latest scan report showed that a rare form of aggressive cancer had invaded her liver. There was no treatment for it, and Barbara's doctor had gently advised her to cancel her motor-home trip and get her affairs in order. The time frame? He guessed Barbara had a few months to live.

"Instead of going on the motor-home adventure I had planned, I am 'going home,'" she explained to me. And then she added, "Alice, this is going to be my fantastic final journey."

And what a truly fantastic journey Barbara has had since then! It has been almost a year instead of the predicted few months. Barbara and I live in different states, but last week we had one more treasured visit together. We sat in her cozy kitchen sharing memories, drinking strong coffee, and eating macaroon cookies that had been dipped in chocolate. She showed me the colorful wall-hanging quilt she had just finished to honor the hospice volunteers caring for her. Then she told me about her plans for a Christmas potluck luncheon where her closest friends would come and decorate her house for the holidays.

I've lost count of the opportunities Barbara has had to speak and write about her adventure of "going home," but many thousands have been touched by what she has to say. The days when she feels fatigued and nauseous are increasing, and she needs a walker and oxygen to get around for longer jaunts—but dear Barbara is still touching lives. And she loves to share a quote that one of her daughters e-mailed her. It has become her slogan:

Life should not be a journey to the grave with the intention of arriving safely in a pretty and well-preserved body, but rather to skid in broadside, thoroughly used up, totally worn out, and loudly proclaiming, "Wow! What a ride!"

You might think Barbara's attitude about dying comes from living an exciting, full life or from her naturally optimistic personality or from the fact that she has not yet come to the most painful stage of her cancer. And you would be partly right. But above all and over all, Barbara's attitude about dying is the same as her attitude about living—she's on a journey of hope. A hope that will not disappoint! A hope that rests on the promises of God. A hope centered in the sacrificial death and resurrection of her Lord and Savior Jesus Christ. A secure hope that her destination is heaven.

Barbara knows that ultimately only God can speak adequately to our needs in times of difficulty. Her journal notes as well as her words of encouragement to others are filled with hope from God's Word. One of the Bible passages that she has turned to again and again during the past few months is Psalm 73:23–26:

> Yet I still belong to you;
>> you are holding my right hand.
> You will keep on guiding me with your counsel,
>> leading me to a glorious destiny.
> Whom have I in heaven but you?
>> I desire you more than anything on earth.
> My health may fail, and my spirit may grow weak,
>> but God remains the strength of my heart;
>> he is mine forever.[1]

Anticipating the Destination

The psalm quoted above says that God is leading us to a glorious destiny, and my friend Barbara has staked her life on that promise. Yet I wonder if most of us are anticipating that destiny as much as she is.

I'm not sure I was . . . until recently.

Of course I had a longing to see my Savior face to face and to be reunited with family and friends who have already arrived on heaven's shores. But I must admit that sometimes, in my heart of hearts, I wondered what we would do for all eternity.

That all changed when I started reading Randy Alcorn's book *Heaven*. Now I can say I'm more excited about my "glorious destiny" than I've ever been before. *Heaven* is a treasure trove of new and thrilling discoveries. It helps the reader picture heaven the way Scripture describes it instead of the way literature and the arts have defined it. Gone are any bland thoughts about floating among the clouds, eternal harp strumming, and never-ending singalongs. These are replaced with biblical descriptions of an exhilarating existence where real people enjoy close relationships with God and each other—eating, working, playing, and worshiping together.

> *Eye has not seen, nor ear heard,*
> *Nor have entered into the heart of man*
> *The things which God has prepared for those who love Him.*
>
> 1 CORINTHIANS 2:9

At one point in his book, Randy Alcorn talks about heaven as home and then reminds us that this isn't simply a metaphor. Heaven is an actual, physical place of comfort and refuge where we will share fabulous food, great conversation, and unprecedented adventures with those we love. It's the one place in God's entire crea-tion where we truly belong.

In the same chapter, Randy talks about the laughter, rejoicing, and celebration that take place in heaven. Here's just one brief excerpt I think you will especially enjoy:

Imagine someone takes you to a party. You see a few friends there, enjoy a couple of good conversations, a little laughter, and some decent appetizers. The party's all right, but you keep hoping it will get better. Give it another hour, and maybe it will. Suddenly, your friend says, "I need to take you home."

Now?

You're disappointed—nobody wants to leave a party early—but you leave, and your friend drops you off at your house. As you open the door and reach for the light switch, you sense someone's there. Your heart's in your throat. You flip on the light.

"Surprise!" Your house is full of smiling people, familiar faces.

It's a party—for you. You smell your favorites—barbecued ribs and pecan pie right out of the oven. The tables are full. It's a feast. You recognize the guests, people you haven't seen for a long time. Then, one by one, the people you most enjoyed at the other party show up at your house, grinning. This turns out to be the real party. You realize that if you'd stayed longer at the other party, as you'd wanted, you wouldn't be at the real party—you'd be away from it.[2]

A few paragraphs later, Randy points out that when someone dies, it's only natural that those left behind will grieve because it feels like someone they loved has left home. In reality, however, Christians aren't leaving home; they're going home. They'll be there before us. The rest of us will just be arriving at the real party a little later.

I like a story I read about a man who, when he realized he was dying, wrote out instructions for a simple memorial service and a request to be buried at a particular spot on the farm where he had lived for years. The memorial service went smoothly until the small community of friends gathered for the graveside service. Since the man hadn't written out any instructions for this part of the service, there was an awkward silence as the adults huddled together to discuss the best way to proceed. While they were trying to decide what to do, a three-year-old girl moved toward the casket and spontaneously began to sing her favorite song, which happened to be "Happy Birthday." I can just imagine the look on the adult faces. I hope they smiled and sang along with her!

In her innocence, this little girl captured the joy of the one who had already gone home to the real party, rather than the sadness of those who would miss him.

Uncertain About the Journey

Maybe you have always been excited about heaven. After all, God is the One who placed eternity in our hearts, and He has promised that He will be there in our midst to wipe all tears from our eyes. You've probably read the descriptions of heaven from the Bible—the foundation layered with precious stones, the gates of pearl, the streets of pure gold. In your mind you can picture the river of life flowing from the throne of God.[3] Most important of all, you know Jesus will be there with open arms to welcome you home. You are looking forward to that glorious destination—but perhaps you are uncertain about the journey, the actual process of dying. Sometimes I'm uncertain too.

None of us knows ahead of time what our death will be like. But it helps me to remember the beloved Twenty-third Psalm, which says,

The LORD is my shepherd;
I shall not want.
He makes me to lie down in green pastures;
He leads me beside the still waters.

He restores my soul. . . .
Yea, though I walk through the valley of the shadow of death,
I will fear no evil;
For You are with me.[4]

What do these familiar words have to say about the experience of death? First, that whether or not our death is difficult, we won't *stay* in the valley of the shadow of death. Death is not a destination; it's just one more place we travel through. More important, the psalm reminds us that we'll never be alone, because our loving Good Shepherd will be right there with us.

We're all somewhere on our journey to death. If we have received Jesus Christ as Savior, we are assured that the journey will take us right to the shores of heaven. Right to the place of ecstatic, eternal joy. One moment we will fall asleep here; the next moment we will wake up there.

Perhaps you are familiar with a gospel song called "The Old Ship of Zion." There are several different versions of it, but they all have the same clear message. The Captain of the ship is Jesus. The destination is Zion, which is another name for heaven. As the Old Ship passes by, the Captain calls out, "Get on board!" And once aboard, the passengers are safe for all eternity. They leave their heartaches and sorrows behind as they sail.

> *The word goodbye will never be used inside heaven's gate.*
> *The word welcome will forever take its place.*
>
> JUDY GORDON

If you have sincerely asked Jesus to be your Savior, rest assured that you are safely on board the ship that will take you home. Your journey on earth may end when you are young or very old, but rest assured that heaven will be your final port of call. (If you are at all uncertain about this, I hope you will read the few pages in the back of this book called "From My Heart to Yours.")

I love the way Henry Van Dyke describes the final voyage:

I am standing upon the seashore. A ship at my side spreads her white sails to the morning breeze and starts for the blue ocean. She is an object of beauty and strength, and I stand and watch until at last she hangs like a speck of white cloud just where the sea and the sky come down to mingle with each other. Then someone at my side says, "There she goes!"

Gone where? Gone from my sight . . . that is all. She is just as large in mast and hull and spar as she was when she left my side and just as able to bear her load of living freight to the place of destination. Her diminished size is in me, not in her. And just at the moment when someone at my side says, "There she goes!" there are other eyes watching her coming and other voices ready to take up the glad shout, "Here she comes!"[5]

We Grieve with Hope

The Bible says that Christians sorrow differently than those who do not have the hope of eternal life.[6] But this doesn't mean we don't grieve when we lose a loved one to death. We, too, have terrible days, sleepless nights, sudden tears, waves of emotion. We, too, have times when we feel like our world is turning upside down. And we never stop missing the ones we love. But still our sorrow is softened, because we know we will see their faces once again.

This past year, a family we love dearly lost their twenty-two-year-old son in an automobile accident. At the memorial service, the pastor read letters written especially for the service by Kevin's dad, mom, sister, and brother. Each one had written something about Kevin's life and how much he had meant to their family. His mother's letter ended with these words: "I shall miss him terribly, but life is short and the memories of him are many. I know we will soon meet in heaven—only a season and a heartbeat away. I eagerly await our heavenly reunion, which will last an eternity."

That's the secret to why we who know Jesus sorrow differently from those who have no hope of heaven. We know their journey has taken them to a new place—one that is better and more wonderful than anything we can imagine here. And we don't have to settle for just the memory of their smile or the touch of their hand because one day we will see their smile again. One day we will walk with them hand in hand again.

When I left Barbara's house last week, we didn't say good-bye. We just opened our arms and threw them around each other for a long, warm hug. I hurried down the walkway blinking my eyes as I tried to keep the tears from spilling down my cheeks. Before reaching the car, I turned around. Barbara was standing on her front porch steps wearing a broad smile, still waving.

Throwing her a kiss, I called out, "I'll see you soon, Barbara! Here, or there, or in the air . . . I'll see you soon."

Only Glimpses

I can't remember when I first heard this story about the young girl who had been blind since birth, but the story is worth retelling. It is a comforting reminder that heaven will be wonderful—truly wonderful.

Laurel knew she was dying. Over the weeks, we talked often about heaven—what it would look like and how it would be to live there. It seemed we always ended up crying, and then holding each other tight.

The hardest part was trying to imagine something we had never seen, something about which we knew only a little.

And then I remembered this story. . . .

The young girl with soft blond hair and eyes the color of sapphire had been blind since birth. Shortly after her twelfth birthday, a new technology was developed, and for the first time her doctor was hopeful that she would be able to see. Several months later, surgery was performed but the bandages could not be removed for two days. Until then, the outcome would be unknown.

The hospital staff brought a small cot into the girl's room so her mother could stay with her through the night. In the darkest hours, the daughter whispered, "Mother, are you awake?"

"Yes, dear, I'm awake."

"Mother, will you tell me again what it will be like when I can see?"

Reaching out in the darkened room, the mother found her daughter's hand. She stroked it softly as she described every lovely thing she could imagine.

Finally the moment came when the bandages were removed. With sobs of joy the young girl saw her mother's gentle face for the first time. She reached up and brushed the tear from her mother's cheek and then traced her finger around her mother's mouth and brow, just as she had done when she was blind. Slowly, with arms wrapped around each other, they crossed the room and looked out the window.

Outside, fluffy white clouds sailed across a sky of faultless blue. Soft breezes stirred the cherry trees, and lacy blossoms sprinkled to the ground like pink snow. Yellow crocuses stood proud along the brick walkway, and a raspberry colored finch fluttered to the edge of a birdbath.

Wonder filling her eyes, the girl turned to her mother.

"Oh, Mother," she whispered, "I never knew it would be so wonderful."

Tears filled my own eyes as I finished the story. I reached for Laurel's hand, not knowing what to say next. It was Laurel who spoke first.

"Right now," she said slowly, "I'm like that young girl in the story—waiting in the darkness, wondering what heaven will look like. Before long . . . I'll be seeing it for real. And with eyes filled with wonder, I'll turn to God and whisper, 'Oh, God, I never knew it would be so wonderful.'"

ALICE GRAY

From *A Gift of Heaven for Every Heart*[7]

A Gentle Touch
For discussion or journaling

Let not your heart be troubled; you believe in God, believe also in Me. In My Father's house are many mansions; if it were not so, I would have told you. I go to prepare a place for you. And if I go and prepare a place for you, I will come again and receive you to Myself; that where I am, there you may be also.

THE WORDS OF JESUS, JOHN 14:1–3

1. Glance back over this chapter. What do you find especially comforting or helpful?

2. Although you probably won't choose "Happy Birthday," do you have other favorite songs or hymns you would like sung at your memorial service? Write a short paragraph that describes how you'd like people to remember you when you say your final good-bye.

3. When you think of heaven, what are you most looking forward to? (For more information about heaven, read chapters 21 and 22 in the book of Revelation.)

A Prayer from the Heart

Dear Lord,

On some bright eternal morning, I will step onto heaven's shore and see You face to face. I'll touch Your nail-scarred hands and feel Your warm embrace as You welcome me home. Friends and loved ones will be there, smiling and laughing for pure joy. It will all be so wonderful.

Oh, thank You, Lord. Thank You for preparing such a glorious place for me. Thank You for all Your blessings. And thank You, Lord, for hope—eternal hope.

Epilogue

From My Heart to Yours

The heart longs for heaven,
heaven longs for the heart.

KIMBER ANNE ENGSTROM

This entire book has been written around the word *hope*. It has been about hope for the storms of life, hope when life has been rearranged by heartache, and hope while we wait for our prayers to be answered. But far more important than any of these is hope for eternal life. And it matters deeply to me that you know that hope for yourself. Yes, I care about what happens in your life now, but I care even more about where you will spend eternity.

Before reading further, please take a moment to read the verses on page 169. Although there are hundreds of verses in the Bible about God's love and His gift of salvation, I chose these from the book of Romans in the New Testament.

If you have never asked Jesus Christ to be your Savior, would you consider inviting Him into your life today? Many years ago, I prayed a simple prayer that went something like this:

Dear Jesus,

I believe that You are the Son of God and that You gave Your life for me on the cross as payment for my sins. I believe that You rose from the dead and that You are alive today in heaven. Please forgive me for my sins and come into my life as Savior and Lord.

Thank You for the gift of eternal life. Help me to obey You and walk with You here on earth until the day when I walk with You in heaven. Amen.

If you have sincerely asked Jesus Christ into your life, He will never leave you. Nothing will be able to separate you from His love. That is a hope you can hang on to in any circumstance, even when all other hope is gone.

God bless you, dear one. I'll look forward to that bright eternal morning when we will meet each other in heaven.

ALICE GRAY

For all have sinned and fall short of the glory of God.

ROMANS 3:23

For the wages of sin is death, but the gift of God is eternal life in Christ Jesus our Lord.

ROMANS 6:23

But God demonstrates His own love toward us, in that while we were still sinners, Christ died for us.

ROMANS 5:8

If you confess with your mouth the Lord Jesus and believe in your heart that God has raised Him from the dead, you will be saved. For with the heart one believes unto righteousness, and with the mouth confession is made unto salvation.

ROMANS 10:9–10

For I am persuaded that neither death nor life, nor angels nor principalities nor powers, nor things present nor things to come, nor height nor depth, nor any other created thing, shall be able to separate us from the love of God which is in Christ Jesus our Lord.

ROMANS 8:38–39

Notes

Prologue: When God Whispers Hope

1. From *Lists to Live By: The Christian Collection*, comp. Alice Gray, Steve Stephens, John Van Diest (Sisters, Oreg.: Multnomah, 2004).

2. The promises in this paragraph are based on four scriptures: Psalm 139:15–16; Romans 8:38–39; Isaiah 40:11; and Psalm 30:5, 11.

3. Emilie Barnes with Anne Christian Buchanan, "A Look Beyond the Clouds," in *Help Me Trust You, Lord* (Eugene, Oreg.: Harvest House, 1998), 141–43.

Chapter 1: Somebody Knows

1. Psalm 46:1–2.

2. Frederick Buechner, *Now and Then: A Memoir of Vocation* (San Francisco: HarperSanFrancisco, 1991).

3. Mark 4:39.

4. Psalm 139:17.

5. New Living Translation.

6. Ron Mehl, *God Works the Night Shift: Acts of Love Your Father Performs Even While You Sleep* (Sisters, Oreg.: Multnomah, 1995), 259–60.

Chapter 2: Picture of Peace

1. Although many versions of this story have been told, I believe the original was by Henry Drummond.

2. M. Scott Peck, *The Road Less Traveled: A New Psychology of Love, Traditional Values and Spiritual Growth*, 25th anniversary edition (New York: Simon & Schuster, Touchstone, 2003), 15. Originally published in 1978.

3. John 16:33.

4. From Philippians 4:7.

5. John 16:33, italics added.

6. The statements in this sentence are based on John 16:33; Psalm 71:5; Revelation 4:8; and Acts 10:36.

7. Isaiah 43:1–2; Matthew 28:20; Romans 8:39, New Living Translation; and Hebrews 13:5.

8. Steve Stephens and Alice Gray, *The Worn Out Woman* (Sisters, Oreg.: Multnomah, 2004). The C-L-O-S-E-R material is condensed from chapter 15, "When Dreams Shatter."

9. Matthew 11:28, New Living Translation.

10. Barbara Johnson, "Spare Parts and Big Feet," in Patsy Clairmont, Barbara Johnson, et al., *Irrepressible Hope: Devotions to Anchor Your Soul and Buoy Your Spirit* (Nashville: W Publishing Group, 2003), 48–51.

Chapter 3: Something Beautiful

1. Taken from a television broadcast. No other source information available.

2. First published in *Century* magazine in 1913. Quoted in John Bartlett, *Familiar Quotations*, 13th ed. (Boston: Little, Brown, 1955), 907.

3. Job 1:21, King James Version.

4. Job 16:1.

5. Job 1:22 and 2:10.

6. C. I. Scofield, *The New Scofield Study Bible* (New York: Oxford University Press, 1988), 712–13 (note keyed to Job 42:6). Scofield's classic and influential study Bible was first published in 1909 and revised by Scofield in 1917.

7. Job 42:17.

8. Billy Graham, "A New Perspective," from *The Secret of Happiness*, in *Billy Graham: The Inspirational Writings* (Nashville: Word Publishing, 1995), 288.

Chapter 4: Blessings

1. I first heard this story in 1988 on a Christian radio program. I've updated the setting and rewritten the story based on the facts I jotted down at the time.

2. 2 Corinthians 4:17–18.

3. Nancy Jo Sullivan, "Bedtime Blessings," from Alice Gray, comp., *Stories for a Woman's Heart: The Second Collection* (Sisters, Oreg.: Multnomah, 2001), 92–94.

Chapter 5: Hush, My Heart

1. Rick Warren, *The Purpose Driven Life* (Grand Rapids, Mich.: Zondervan, 2002), 90.

2. New International Version.

3. Taken from "His Eye Is on the Sparrow" on Cyber Hymnal Web site, http://www.cyberhymnal.org/htm/h/i/hiseyeis.htm. Accessed 31 January 2005.

4. John thomas Oaks, "The Sparrow at Starbucks," *Christian Reader*, November/December 2001, 11. Note: *Christian Reader* is now *Today's Christian* magazine.

5. Joanna Bloss, "Spiritually Dry," *Virtue*, December 1999/January 2000, 51.

Chapter 6: Cushions of Comfort

1. Robert Louis Stevenson, "The Swing," in *A Child's Garden of Verses*, rev. ed., illus. Tasha Tudor (New York: Simon & Schuster Children's Publishing, 1999), 36.

2. Nancy Stafford, *The Wonder of His Love* (Sisters, Oreg.: Multnomah, 2004), 67–68.

3. Ruth Graham, *In Every Pew Sits a Broken Heart* (Grand Rapids, Mich.: Zondervan, 2004), 11.

4. Ibid., 142.

5. Joni Eareckson Tada, *A Step Further* (Grand Rapids, Mich.: Zondervan, 1978), 14.

6. Warren, *Purpose Driven Life*, 246–247.

7. Mayo Mathers, "The Comfort Room," *Today's Christian Woman*, November/December 1996, reprinted in Alice Gray, comp., *Stories for the Heart, Third Collection* (Sisters, Oreg.: Multnomah, 1996), 78–81.

Chapter 7: When Parents Cry

1. James Dobson, *Parenting Isn't for Cowards: Dealing Confidently with the Frustrations of Child-Rearing* (Dallas, Tex: Word, 1988), 49.

2. Ruth Bell Graham, *Prodigals: And Those Who Love Them* (Grand Rapids, Mich.: Baker, 1999), 13.

3. "Listen, Lord," also called "A Mother Is Praying," in Graham, *Prodigals*, 35. Used by permission.

4. New Living Translation.

5. Philip D. Yancey, *What's So Amazing About Grace?* (Grand Rapids, Mich.: Zondervan, 1997), 49–51.

Chapter 8: Heartbreak Hill

1. John Claypool, *The Hopeful Heart* (Harrisburg, Pa.: Morehouse, 2003), 53.

2. Hebrews 12:1–3, New American Standard Version.

3. From Carole Mayhall, *Lord, Teach Me Wisdom* (Colorado Springs: NavPress, 1979), 147–48.

4. Psalm 145:18 and Isaiah 40:11.

Chapter 9: Held in God's Hands

1. Eva Marie Everson, "Mandy's Ministry," in Alice Gray, comp., *Stories for the Extreme Teen's Heart* (Sisters, Oreg.: Multnomah, 2000), 208–11. You can access Mandy's Web site at www.pray4mandy.com.

2. James Dobson, *When God Doesn't Make Sense* (Wheaton, Ill.: Tyndale House, 1993), 88–89.

3. Jennifer Rothschild, "From Jennifer: Longing to Kneel," in *Women's Ministry eNewsletter*, Issue #237 (28 October 2004), www.womensministry.net. Accessed at http://groups.yahoo.com/group/womensministry-news/message/274, 1 February 2005.

4. Isaac Watts, "Alas! And Did My Savior Bleed?" on www.cyberhymnal.org, accessed at http://www.cyberhymnal.org/htm/a/l/alasand.htm, 31 January 2005.

5. Joni Eareckson Tada, *Glorious Intruder: God's Presence in Life's Chaos* (Sisters, Oreg.: Multnomah, 1989), 189–91.

Chapter 10: Journey of Hope

1. New Living Translation.

2. Randy Alcorn, *Heaven* (Wheaton, Ill.: Tyndale House, 2004), 441–42.

3. See Ecclesiastes 3:11; Isaiah 25:8; Revelation 21:3–4, 18–21; and 22:1–2.

4. Psalm 23:1–4.

5. This piece by the well-known poet and educator, often titled "A Parable of Immortality," is widely quoted—with many variations. This version, which appeared to me to be most authentic, can be found on the Sea Services Web site: http://www.seaservices.com/prayers.htm#beecher.

6. 1 Thessalonians 4:13–18.

7. Alice Gray, *A Gift of Heaven for Every Heart* (Sisters, Oreg.: Multnomah, 2002), 35–38.

Permissions

"God Is There," by Dr. Steve Stephens, from *Lists to Live By: The Christian Collection*, comp. Alice Gray, Steve Stephens, John Van Diest (Sisters, Oreg.: Multnomah, 2004). Used by permission of the author.

"A Look Beyond the Clouds," by Emilie Barnes. Taken from *Help Me Trust You, Lord*, by Emilie Barnes with Anne Christian Buchanan. Copyright © 2000 by Harvest House Publishers, Eugene, Oreg. Used by permission.

"Even If It's Dark," by Ron Mehl. Excerpted from *When God Works the Night Shift*, © 1994 by Ron Mehl. Used by permission of Multnomah Publishers, Inc.

"Spare Parts and Big Feet," by Barbara Johnson. Reprinted by permission. *Irrepressible Hope: Devotions to Anchor Your Soul and Buoy Your Spirit*, by Patsy Clairmont, Barbara Johnson, Nicole Johnson, Marilyn Meberg, Luci Swindoll, Sheila Walsh, Thelma Wells, © 2003, W Publishing, a Division of Thomas Nelson, Inc., Nashville, Tennessee. All rights reserved.

"A New Perspective," by Billy Graham. Reprinted by permission. *The Secret of Happiness*, by Billy Graham, © 1995, W Publishing Group, a Division of Thomas Nelson, Inc., Nashville, Tennessee. All rights reserved.

"Bedtime Blessings," by Nancy Jo Sullivan, originally published in *Stories for a Woman's Heart: The Second Collection*. Used by permission of the author.

"The Sparrow at Starbucks," by John thomas Oaks, as printed in *Christian Reader*, November/December 2001, vol. 39, no. 6, 11, copyright © 2001 John thomas Oaks. Used by permission of the author.

About the Author

Alice Gray is best known for her six million copy best-selling series, "Stories for the Heart," which has won her many awards and honors. An inspirational conference speaker and radio and television guest, Alice has been inspiring women for more than two decades. She is a mother and a grandmother and lives with her husband, Al, in Arizona.

BE SURE TO LOOK FOR THESE UPCOMING BOOKS IN THE

Treasures for Women Series

by best-selling author Alice Gray

Treasures for Women Who Make a Difference	Summer 2006
Treasures for Women Who Love God	Spring 2007
Treasures for Women Who Pray	Winter 2007
Treasures for Women Who Forgive	Fall 2008
Treasures for Women Who Become Beautiful	Summer 2009

"My vision is to help women become who God had in mind when He created them. I pray these books will encourage you to make those daily choices of the heart that will ultimately change your life!"

— ALICE GRAY

W PUBLISHING GROUP
A Division of Thomas Nelson Publishers
Since 1798

For other life-changing resources, visit us at:
www.thomasnelson.com